Domestic Rabbit Biology
and Production

Domestic Rabbit Biology and Production

Lewis

L. R. Arrington

K. C. Kelley

A UNIVERSITY OF FLORIDA BOOK

THE UNIVERSITY PRESSES OF FLORIDA
GAINESVILLE / 1976

Library of Congress Cataloging in Publication Data

Arrington, Lewis R   1919–
    Domestic rabbit biology and production.

    "A University of Florida book."
    Includes index.
    1. Rabbits. I. Kelley, K. C., 1938–   joint
author. II. Title.
SF453.A66   636'.93'22   76–10173
ISBN 0-8130-0537-X

Figures 7.1–7.4 copyright © 1971 by Kathleen C. Kelley.

PRINTED BY ROSE PRINTING CO., TALLAHASSEE, FLORIDA

CONTENTS

PREFACE

Domestic rabbits are produced in virtually all countries of the world for a number of different purposes. Most are raised for food, many are produced and used for research, and others are maintained for pleasure as pets or fancy animals. This diversity of objectives and interests indicates the need for communication and publication of information useful to individuals or groups with varied interests in rabbits.

This book is designed and presented as a general volume on domestic rabbits. It is not intended only as a biology book or as one concerned primarily with practical production; elements of both subjects are included. The objectives have been to record, in a brief volume, a balance of basic and applied information on various subjects relating to rabbits and to provide additional sources of information through references listed. Complete details of every subject which may be of interest to each reader could not be included, but the authors hope that useful information is presented for those with diverse interests in rabbits.

In the preparation of this manuscript, the authors have had valuable help from many individuals, and this assistance is acknowledged with sincere thanks. Dr. D. E. Franke was primarily responsible for the chapter on genetics and animal improvement; Dr. G. A. Olson made valuable suggestions and contributed to the chapter on diseases; and Dr. W. K. Mathis contributed information for the chapter on economics and marketing. Other officials and colleagues of The Institute of Food and Agricultural Sciences of the University of Florida made suggestions and expressed interest and encouragement. Credit is due Frances C. Arrington for editorial assistance and for typing portions of the manuscript and T. C. Beaty for assistance with illustrations.

1. INTRODUCTION

The domestic rabbit (*Oryctolagus cuniculus*) has been associated with man and has contributed to his well-being for many centuries. It is used as food, as an experimental subject in research, for fur, and is a source of much pleasure as a pet and fancy animal. The rabbit adapts to a great variety of environmental conditions and is found in the wild and domesticated state on every continent. It is the most widely hunted of the wild game. The folklore of many lands includes stories about and references to rabbits and hares. There are more breeds and varieties of domestic rabbits than of any other animal except the dog.

This book is concerned with the different breeds and varieties of the domesticated European rabbit. Relationships to the other genera and species will be noted in the following chapter.

Domestic rabbits are raised in every state in the United States and in most of the counties of each. The total number of producers is about 150,000. Statistics are not available to indicate the exact numbers raised annually in this country but the estimate is 5 to 7 million for all purposes. Commercial slaughter for meat accounts for about 2 million and an equal or slightly smaller number are slaughtered for noncommercial or home use. Research laboratories use 500,000 to 800,000 per year, and those kept as pets or fancy animals amount to several hundred thousand. Annual consumption of rabbit meat is about 8 to 10 million pounds of which 1 to 2 million pounds are imported from foreign countries.

Peak production in this country was reached in 1944 when it

1

was estimated that 24 million rabbits were raised. In times of national emergency, such as during both world wars, and in other periods of food shortages and high prices, rabbit production has traditionally increased. Expanded production can provide an increased amount of high quality protein for the family and add variety to the diet. The rabbit is herbivorous, subsisting in part on roughage type feeds which are generally less expensive than concentrates. The rabbit should continue to have a place as a meat-producing animal, and in times of feed shortage its value should increase because of its ability to utilize some roughage feeds.

Rabbit production as an industry is small when compared to the amount of meat produced in and monetary income derived from poultry and the other livestock industries. However, its importance must not be evaluated only on this basis. Contributions to research, pleasure provided to owners of pets and fancy animals, and the value in youth projects make rabbit raising far more beneficial and significant than its economic value alone. Most rabbit production units are small; thus, many individuals and families are involved. The total number of families raising rabbits and in part dependent upon them as a source of food and income is very large.

Domestic rabbits are raised extensively in Great Britain and other western European countries. The European rabbit, from which domestic breeds were developed, also exists in the wild state and some are trapped or slaughtered for meat. Before World War II, the rabbit population in England was estimated to be about 50 million. By 1950 it had increased to an estimated 60–100 million, but in 1953–54, the myxomatosis virus killed a majority of the wild rabbits in Britain. About 200 million rabbits are produced annually in France, and consumption there amounts to approximately 6 kilograms or 13 pounds of meat per person per year.

The capital investment needed to begin raising rabbits is not large when compared to that needed by most other livestock industries. The amount of land, equipment, and other items required is relatively small. Since the space required is not large, it is often possible to raise rabbits near the home on rather small acreage.

In some parts of the world introduced rabbits have escaped into the wild state and have multiplied rapidly when there were insufficient natural enemies. They became serious pests by consuming and destroying certain vegetable crops cultivated for human food. In some areas there has been such destruction that debates arose concerning whether or not rabbits were desirable animals and consideration was given to control measures.

PRODUCTION PURPOSES

MEAT

Most domestic rabbits produced in this country are slaughtered for food. Rabbit meat is of high quality, all white, appealing, and tasty. The industry is based primarily on the sale of 8-week-old rabbits, referred to as fryers. Most are medium-weight breeds, and the young are sold when they weigh about 3-3/4–4-3/4 pounds and are 7–9 weeks old. The dressing percentage of good quality rabbits is about 60 per cent so the carcasses weigh about 2 pounds. Rabbit meat may be cooked in a number of ways, and traditionally it has been prepared in most of the same ways as has poultry. The meat of younger or fryer age rabbits is quite tender. Older or mature rabbits, usually referred to as roasters, may also be sold for meat. As is the case with most other food animals, the mature ones are less tender than the young ones.

Although production of rabbits for meat is a comparatively small industry, it is large enough for commercial production and slaughtering in many areas. The large-scale producer may operate his own slaughtering house or processing plant. Small production units that cannot justify the operation of a slaughtering (processing) plant would normally sell to a nearby processor or market through a cooperative. The processor may periodically pick up the marketable rabbits from nearby producers, or producers may deliver their rabbits to his plant. Systems for marketing rabbits are not as well established or as well organized as are those for some other types of animals, and the methods may vary considerably in different locations. The very small-scale producers or family units raising a few rabbits frequently slaughter their own rabbits for individual use.

In many sections of the country and in many specific areas within states, substantial markets for rabbit meat have been established. In other areas, rabbit meat may not be seen regularly in the supermarket or in other meat sales outlets. When high quality rabbit meat is made available consistently and routinely, these markets usually exist. The probable reason that rabbit is seldom seen in certain areas is that uniform, good quality rabbit meat has not been made available, and the consumer, therefore, has not become accustomed to utilizing this high quality meat.

RESEARCH AND LABORATORY

Several species of small animals including rabbits are used in large numbers as research subjects. As medical and biological experimentation have increased in recent years, the production of animals for this purpose has become a sizeable and specialized industry. Many of these small animals have made significant contributions to scientific development. The domestic rabbit has been and continues to be used in a variety of experiments. The research which ultimately led to the cure for diphtheria was carried out largely with rabbits, and this species was the first animal model used in atherosclerosis research. In the past rabbits were used extensively in pregnancy tests, but newer methods have been developed and their use for this purpose has declined significantly. Rabbits are used in a variety of physiological, disease, nutritional, and other types of studies. The unique characteristic of induced ovulation and the habitual practice of coprophagy (eating of feces) are of special importance in certain types of research. The use of rabbits in research is not limited to these unique features. Although some studies are carried out more efficiently with rabbits than with other animals, some studies require rabbits. They possess many characteristics similar to other species of mammals, so they may be used in comparative studies. The cost, size, and availability of the rabbit are of importance to the research worker.

Currently about 600,000 rabbits are used in research annually; only mice, rats, guinea pigs, and hamsters are used in larger numbers. The New Zealand White rabbit has been most widely used for many years. Many of the biological and physiological constants of this breed have been established, and scientists are often reluctant to change to others. Currently there is interest in using the smaller breeds which require less feed, need smaller cages, and mature earlier. When more detailed physiological and biological data for these breeds are established, no doubt their use in research will increase.

There is a market demand for rabbits as laboratory animals, and some producers raise them only for this purpose. This is a specialized market, however, and it does not mean that anyone who has a few spare rabbits can expect to market them successfully for research. Those producers who can supply animals of the necessary quality and type can usually find suitable and rewarding markets. Requirements of the laboratory animal market are different from the meat market, and the needs of the laboratory are often difficult for the small producer to meet. Laboratory animals must be as uniform as possible in terms of genetic background, age, sex, and other characteristics. Frequently a large number of rabbits with specific characteristics may be required at one time. Additional information on this topic is included in subsequent sections.

SHOW AND FANCY

Some people are interested in and produce rabbits entirely for the pleasure of breeding and showing fancy animals. There are a number of breeds which are considered fancy breeds and are seldom used for other purposes. Rabbit clubs and associations have been formed in many parts of the country, and these clubs promote regular meetings and schedule shows, which not only provide pleasure and a means of exchanging information, but also provide an incentive for genetic improvement and good quality rabbit production. Considerable competition can be generated in the production of rabbits for exhibit in such shows.

YOUTH PROJECTS

Not the least of the contributions made by rabbits is their value in various youth projects. These include Scouts, 4-H clubs, Future Farmers of America, and high school science projects. The educational benefits to be derived from these projects is varied. Many aspects of biology, including reproduction, can be studied, and youngsters of various ages can learn the responsibility of caring for animals. If rabbits are sold at the termination of a project, some economic principles may be learned from computation of costs of feed, labor, and other necessities.

MISCELLANEOUS USES

Associated with the production of rabbits for show and fancy is the pleasure they provide as pets to both young and old. They are especially popular at Easter. Rabbits are not considered household pets in the same way as are dogs and cats, but they can be valuable pets. Such rabbits should be caged or penned, not only to prevent their escape, but to protect them from dogs and other predators. The types of housing described in subsequent sections can be used or modified for pet housing. Rabbits adapt well to the type of care and frequent handling normally given to pets. Proper feeding, disease prevention, and housing must be considered. It is unlikely that persons keeping rabbits for pets would also be involved in their production for meat.

Pelt production is not a primary objective in raising rabbits, but rabbit furs are used in the manufacture of clothing and toys and can be readily processed to provide material for many attractive objects. Pelts from some breeds are prized for making coats, gloves, and other items, and those from the slaughter of fryer rabbits are generally used in the manufacture of felt. A rabbit foot is considered a good luck charm, and key chains and other objects are made from rabbit feet and skins.

Angora wool is produced by rabbits of that breed. This "wool" or hair makes a very fine fabric which is highly prized. However, with the advent of many synthetic fabrics, the production of angora wool in this country is now very limited.

The volume of slaughterhouse waste from rabbits does not normally justify processing, although some waste is used in processed dog food and for feeding zoo animals. The blood and various organs and tissues may be removed, frozen or otherwise specially processed, and sold for research or laboratory purposes.

Domestic rabbits have occasionally been used to train greyhounds for racing The practice is now considered inhumane and certainly should be discouraged. Laws preventing it have been passed in several states.

HISTORICAL NOTES

Detailed and accurate records of the early history of the rabbit are difficult to locate. Its light, fragile bones do not preserve well, so fossil evidence is limited. It appears certain that after the end of the last glacial period, the rabbit was found only on the Iberian Peninsula. *Oryctolagus cuniculus* (L.), forerunner of all domestic rabbits, was originally in Spain only but soon spread to other western Mediterranean countries and Europe. The European rabbit, from which all domestic breeds derive, originated in countries of the western Mediterranean.

The Greek historian Polybius, in writing of Corsica during the second century BC, was apparently the first to refer to the present European rabbit. He noted that there were no hares on the island, but there were some burrowing animals resembling small hares which he called *kunikloi*. The introduction of the rabbit to Corsica has an uncertain source. Rabbits were not known to the classical Greeks, but hares were, and there are references to hunting and to snares.

Rabbits probably entered human history when the Phoenicians reached the shores of Spain. They were impressed with the abundance of small, burrowing animals like the hyrax of their own country. The name for hyrax in Semitic tongues is *shephan*, and they gave the name *I-shephan-im* to the newly discovered shore. The latinized form of this term is Hispania. Coins from the reign of the Emperor Hadrian (117–138 AD), found in Spain, depict the rabbit. Rabbits are not mentioned in the Bible, but references to hares appear in Leviticus 11:6 and Deuteronomy 14:7. The hare, a close relative, is listed in the Hebrew dietary laws as one of the animals forbidden to be eaten. These citations in the Old Testament refer to the hare as an animal which chews its cud, although neither the hare nor the rabbit chews cud. It is not understood why the description was used, but it may have resulted from the appearance of chewing the cud in normal eating. There is no evidence that the reference is to some other animal. References to the coney in Psalms 104:18 and Proverbs 30:26 (Authorized Version) refer not to the rabbit but to the hyrax or badger and are so indicated in later translations. The Hebrew word *shofon*, which means hyrax, was translated as coney (rabbit) in several versions of the Bible.

It is difficult to designate a specific time or place when it can be said that rabbits were domesticated. The time must have been rather late, however, in view of the wide distribution and the ease with which they may be bred and maintained in captivity. Records of domestication prior to the Middle Ages are not clear, but it is known that rabbits were kept in captivity in Roman times. The Roman scholar and author Varro (116–27 BC) suggested that rabbits be kept in leporaria. Domestication as we know it was likely accomplished by monks in medieval times. Newborn and unborn rabbits were eaten during Lent, and the need to maintain pregnant does in enclosures provided an impetus for maintenance of rabbits under domesticated conditions. Stone walls usually provided the necessary enclosure in ancient times, but then and more recently, some rabbits were maintained by confinement on rabbit islands.

Domestic rabbits were not known in Britain before Norman times, but definite records of their presence appeared in the thirteenth century. By the sixteenth century they were clearly abundant in England, and in the seventeenth century many estates had rabbit warrens.

Color variants were not noted in rabbits until about the middle of the sixteenth century. The earliest evidence of a white rabbit is in the painting *Madonna with the Rabbit* by Titian, about 1550.

Domestic rabbits in this country were derived from the European rabbit and not from existing wild species. Records of the early introduction of the European rabbit into America are scarce. It is assumed that the animals were brought by the early settlers, and it appears they were maintained for the same purposes then as they are now. Several of the breeds and varieties now recognized by the American Rabbit Breeders Association (ARBA) in the United States were developed here.

European rabbits exist in many countries as domestic breeds and in the wild. The spread of tame and wild rabbits occurred separately and independently. Often the tame animals were present prior to the appearance of the wild ones.

The term "rabbit" (rabbet, rabbyt, rabette) was not applied to animals of all ages until the eighteenth century. Prior to that adults were known as conies, and only the young were called rabbits. The species name *cuniculus* means underground passage in Latin, and European rabbits in the wild state spend most of the day in underground tunnels. The word for rabbit in many European languages derives from *cuniculus*: *conejo* in Spanish; *kaninchen* in German; *connin* in Old French; *coniglio* in Italian; and *conyng* and *coney* in Old English. The term "bunny" is a diminutive of the word "bun" which possibly refers to the rabbit tail.

The association of rabbits with Easter comes from pagan antiquity. Early Easter festivals were related to ideas of new life, periodicity, and fertility. In ancient Egypt the hare was a symbol of fertility; the rabbit has replaced the hare in this symbolism. The most popular symbolism associated with the rabbit and hare is that related to reproduction. Several unusual characteristics such as a bisexual nature and the ability to reproduce without mating were attributed to the hare. Origin of the myth regarding rabbits laying eggs is unknown.

REFERENCES

Adams, C. E. 1972. The rabbit. In *The UFAW Handbook on the Care and Management of Laboratory Animals.* Williams and Wilkins Co.: Baltimore, Maryland.

American Rabbit Breeders Association. 1972. *Official Guide to Raising Better Rabbits.* American Rabbit Breeders Association: Bloomington, Illinois.

Casady, R. B., P. B. Sawin, and J. Van Dam. 1971. Commercial rabbit raising. Agriculture Handbook 309. U.S. Department of Agriculture: Washington, D.C.

Caveny, D. D., and H. L. Enos. 1972. A bibliography of the domestic rabbit. Bulletin 481a. Cooperative Ext. Serv., Colorado State Univ.: Ft. Collins.

Faivre, M. I. 1973. *How to Raise Rabbits for Fun and Profit.* Nelson-Hall Co.: Chicago, Illinois.

Makepiece, L. I. 1956. Rabbits: A subject bibliography. Colorado State Univ. Multigraph Service: Ft. Collins.

Murgatroyd, A. E. 1972. Pounds, rabbits and sense. Vet. Rec. 91: 596–98.

Naether, C. A. 1967. *The Book of the Domestic Rabbit.* David McKay Co.: New York.

Napier, R. A. N. 1963. Rabbits. In *Animals for Research*, ed. W. Lane-Petter. Academic Press: New York.

Netherway, M. E. P. 1973. *A Manual of Rabbit Farming.* Fur and Feather: Idle, Bradford, England.

Sandford, J. C. 1957. *The Domestic Rabbit.* Crosby Lockwood: London.

Sheail, J. 1971. *Rabbits and Their History.* David and Charles, Ltd.: Newton Abbot, Devon, England.

Templeton, G. S. 1968. *Domestic Rabbit Production.* The Interstate Printers and Publishers: Danville, Illinois.

Thompson, H. V., and A. N. Worden. 1956. *The Rabbit.* Collins: London.

United States Department of Agriculture. 1972. Selecting and raising rabbits. Agriculture Information Bulletin 358. Washington, D.C.

2. THE DOMESTIC RABBIT

The purpose of this chapter is to present general information on the rabbit and on its taxonomic classification and relation to similar species, and to identify and describe the various breeds of domestic rabbits.

The rabbit belongs to the class Mammalia, order Lagomorpha, and family Leporidae. Its young are born in a fur-lined nest and are blind, helpless, and without hair at birth. The term "domestic rabbit" generally refers to tame rabbits maintained in cages, pens, or other enclosures, and are thus distinguished from the similar and closely related rabbits existing in the natural or wild state. All of the breeds and varieties of domestic rabbits were developed from the European rabbit (*Oryctolagus cuniculus*). In some parts of the world, however, European rabbits exist in the wild state so the term "domestic" must refer to those maintained in close relation to man. In this country, the wild rabbits and hares belong to different genera and species. European or domestic rabbits are not native to the United States.

The numerous breeds and varieties of domestic rabbits vary widely in size, color, type of fur, and other characteristics. These variations may give the impression that there are greater differences between breeds than really exist. Since they were all developed by selective breeding of the European rabbit, the basic characteristics of domestic rabbits in terms of anatomy, physiology, nutritional needs, and diseases are similar. Different breed characteristics such as size and type of hair coat make possible the selection of a particular breed for a particular production purpose. The development of many breeds and types represents an example of the application of genetics and breeding techniques to the improvement of animals to serve mankind.

Domestic rabbits may be raised in virtually all of the climatic conditions of the temperate zone. When protected from rain and wind they can tolerate temperatures well below freezing. If temperatures are consistently above 90°F they suffer from the heat; males become less fertile, and decreased performance in terms of growth and reproduction results. Mortality frequently occurs at prolonged temperatures of 95°F or higher. In locations with either extreme in climatic conditions, adjustments or modifications in housing should be made to provide as much protection as possible.

BEHAVIOR

In the natural or wild state, the European rabbit lives in groups in meadows, in lightly wooded areas, or on edges of woods. Most of the day is spent in a series of complex underground tunnels and passages. Native American wild rabbits do not dig tunnels, although they normally remain hidden most of the day. Feeding and other activities take place in the late afternoon or at night. The European rabbit has adapted well to the conditions of confinement required in housing domestic rabbits, although under these conditions some of the natural characteristics and behavioral patterns may not be so readily observed. When domestic rabbits are closely confined the adults will fight excessively and should be penned individually. Rabbits in well-managed colonies are seldom aggressive toward humans with the exception of those with young or a few that have nervous temperaments. If such behavior occurs, it is manifested as rushing and pawing with the forefeet, accompanied by a slight growl-hissing noise; they seldom cause injury. Generally, rabbits will not bite a person, but they will bite and slash each other with the incisor teeth when fighting. Injury will usually occur as a scratch in handling, but if the animals are handled properly, scratching and clawing can be avoided.

Rabbits are generally quite calm in rabbitries, and adults will lie calmly in their cages most of the day. In the late afternoon or near feeding time, activity increases. About 75 per cent of the total daily feed and water is consumed at night. Rabbits are normally very quiet and vocal noises are seldom heard. The noise of pain or extreme excitement is a high-pitched squeal. They are easily frightened and sudden loud noises or the sudden appearance of a strange person or a strange object may frighten them to the extent that they will panic and run wildly in the cages for several minutes. The panic of one seems to spread almost immediately to others and usually all within a house are affected, although it may be limited to a localized area of the building. This activity is so rapid and wild that injuries can occur.

Foot stamping is frequently observed as a result of excitement or fear, and it may be assumed to be a signal or warning to others. Both rear feet are used simultaneously to pound the ground or cage floor with heavy blows, usually several seconds apart. The movement is so rapid that it is seldom seen except on close observation, but the noise is clearly heard. Since the movement is difficult to see, the origin of the noise may puzzle the beginning rabbit raiser. It normally occurs in males immediately after mating, but it is also a reaction to fear or excitement in both sexes. Rabbits that are nervous or excitable and exhibit excessive foot stamping may be expected to have more problems with sore hocks than do others (chapter 7).

TAXONOMIC CLASSIFICATION

In order to identify the domestic rabbit adequately and relate it to other rabbits and animals, it is necessary to review taxonomic classification. All animals and plants are classified by this system which provides certain basic information on their similarities and differences and also assigns a universally applied scientific name which should be used for accurate identification. The domestic rabbit is classified as follows:

Kingdom—Animalia
  Phylum—Chordata (presence of notochord, skeletal axis)
    Subphylum—Vertebrata (backbone)
      Class—Mammalia (body hair, suckle young, 4-chambered
          heart, warm-blooded, young born live)
        Order—Lagomorpha (pikas, rabbits, hares)
          Family—Leporidae (rabbits and hares)
            Genus—*Oryctolagus* (European rabbit)
              Species—*cuniculus* (underground passage)
                Breeds
                  Varieties
                  Strains

Some older definitions classified the rabbit as a rodent, but it is no longer placed in the order Rodentia. It does possess chisel-like or gnawing teeth similar to those of rodents, but the rabbit has two upper and two lower incisor teeth as well as two smaller pulp teeth behind the upper incisors, making a total of six rather than four as is characteristic of rodents. Certain blood characteristics were also found to be different from those of rodents, so rabbits are now classified in the order Lagomorpha. Within this order there are two families: Ochotonidae (the pikas, sometimes called conies) and Leporidae (the rabbits and hares). All Lagomorphs are herbivorous.

Pikas are smaller than rabbits, with short ears and a small tail that is not externally visible. They normally inhabit the cold, mountainous regions of North America and Asia.

Members of the Leporidae inhabit most of the temperate regions of the world. Their ears are longer and wider than those of pikas and they are generally larger animals, although there is a wide range in the size of rabbits and hares. Hares differ from rabbits in that they are born fully haired, with their eyes open, and they are able to run within a few minutes after birth. Their legs are longer than those of rabbits and they take long leaps in running. Young are born in the open without a nest. The term "hare" is generally applied to any Lagomorph with these characteristics, and this distinguishes them from rabbits.

Some of the more common wild rabbits and hares are:
    Lepus arcticus, Arctic hare
    L. americanus, snowshoe or varying hare
    L. californicus, black-tailed jackrabbit
    Sylvilagus aquaticus, swamp rabbit
    S. bachmani, brush rabbit
    S. floridanus, eastern cottontail.

Some animals called hares are not hares but rabbits, and some called rabbits are actually hares. The jackrabbit in this country is not a rabbit but a hare, and the Belgian Hare, one of the larger breeds, is a rabbit.

BREEDS

Thirty-eight breeds and eighty-nine varieties of domestic rabbits are recognized by the American Rabbit Breeders Association (ARBA). Several breeds and a number of the varieties were developed in this country, but most originated in Western Europe. Breeds of rabbits and other animals may be developed by one or a combination of several methods. Animals from different established breeds may be mated and the offspring selected for desirable characteristics sought in the new breed. Sometimes several different breeds contribute to the formation of the new breed. Other breeds may be formed or initiated through genetic changes (mutations) which occasionally occur spontaneously and result in animals which are in some ways different from their parents and from their immediate ancestors. If these new animals possess characteristics thought to be desirable, they may be mated and the offspring selected and bred. The selection and breeding of two animals with desirable characteristics from nonestablished breeds may lead to the development of a new breed. The various breeds and varieties of domestic rabbits were developed by one of these methods. Some of the breeds of rabbits were developed many years ago when the laws of genetic inheritance were not as well understood as they are today. Considerable credit should be given to the early developers and pioneers who worked without benefit of the present knowledge of genetic inheritance.

In order for a new genetic line of rabbits to be recognized as a breed, it must meet certain standards established by an agency or organization concerned with breed standards. In this country the ARBA serves this function. It maintains breed standards, establishes rules or guidelines by which new breeds are recognized, and provides a registry for purebred animals.

The different breeds are grouped into small, medium, and large weight classes as a general classification of size. Another type of classification distinguishes the fancy breeds from the commercial ones. Fancy breeds are those produced and maintained primarily for show and exhibition; commercial breeds are those produced primarily for sale as meat or for other economic purposes.

A third classification is often made on the basis of the type of fur structure: normal, rex, and satin. The coat consists of two types of hair: undercoat hair which gives density to the fur and longer and coarser guard hairs which give texture. Variations in these structures account for the different types of fur. Normal fur is that with a dense undercoat and longer guard hairs typical of most rabbits. In rex fur, the guard hairs are not longer than the undercoat and there is no flyback. The coat is soft and produces the most valuable type of commercial fur. Satin fur results from a modification of the guard hairs which gives the coat a sheen, a satin-like texture, and a very desirable appearance. The rex and satin type furs developed as genetic mutations. The rex mutation first appeared about 1919 in France and the satin in 1930 in the United States. These fur types have been introduced into other breeds, thus producing a number of varieties.

The specific genetic background for many breeds of rabbits is not known. In some cases, the breeds used to develop a new breed are known, but the proportion or percentage of each background is not. The following descriptions present limited information on the origin and general characteristics of the different breeds. Additional information may be obtained from the publications "Standard of Perfection" and "Official Guide to Raising Better Rabbits" of the ARBA (present address: 2401 E. Oakland

Ave., Bloomington, Illinois 61701) and other references listed at the end of the chapter.

Certain terms are frequently used to describe the different types of fur and other characteristics of rabbits. The more common terms are defined below.

Flyback—the property of fur which causes it to flow back quickly and evenly to its normal position when stroked toward the head.

Ticking—a wavy distribution of longer guard hair throughout the fur of a color distinct from the underwool or body fur. Ticking is usually produced by black-tipped guard hairs, as in Flemish Giants and Belgian Hares.

Selfs—animals with the same color fur on the entire body.

Charlies—animals with lightly marked color patterns.

Cobby—stout, compact, stocky, short legs, and short body.

Mandolin—as applied to type, having the appearance of an inverted mandolin; back and saddle arching toward the loin to make noticeably large and broad hindquarters.

A discussion of the thirty-eight breeds of domestic rabbits found in the United States follows in alphabetical order with no grouping as to type, characteristics, importance, or use. Registration weights for the various breeds are given in Table 2.1.

ALASKA

This breed was recognized by the ARBA in 1975. Weight classification places it between the small and medium breeds with an ideal of 7-1/2 pounds for both does and bucks. Body type is slightly cobby with heavy shoulders and slightly broader and higher rear quarters. The dense, medium-length fur is glossy black on the surface, blending into a slate blue undercoat near the skin; it has typical flyback and guard hairs slightly coarser than the undercoat.

AMERICAN

Two varieties are recognized in this country: Blue and White. The American Blue was imported into the United States in the early 1900s and first exhibited around 1917. Its fur is a dark slate

TABLE 2.1. Breeds, Varieties, and Registration Weights

Breed	No. Varieties (Colors)	Does		Bucks	
		lbs	kg	lbs	kg
Alaska	1	6.5–8.5	3.0–3.9	6.5–8.5	3.0–3.9
American	2	10–12	4.5–5.4	9–11	4.1–5.0
Angora (English)	2	5.5–8.0	2.5–3.6	5.25–7.5	2.4–3.4
Angora (French)	2	7 or over	3.2	7 or over	3.2
Belgian Hare	1	6–9	2.7–4.1	6–9	2.7–4.1
Bevern	3	9–11	4.1–5.0	8–10	3.6–4.5
Blue Vienna	1	9–11.5	4.1–5.2	8–10.5	3.6–4.8
Californian	1	8.5–10.5	3.9–4.8	8–10	3.6–4.5
Champagne d'Argent	1	9.5–12.0	4.3–5.4	9–11	4.1–5.0
Checkered Giant (American)	2	12 or over	5.4	11 or over	5.0
Chinchilla (American)	1	10–12	4.5–5.4	9–11	4.1–5.0
Chinchilla (Giant)	1	13–16	5.9–7.3	12–15	5.4–6.8
Chinchilla (Standard)	1	6–8	2.7–3.6	5.5–7.5	2.5–3.4
Cinnamon	1	9–11	4.1–5.0	8.5–10.5	3.9–4.8
Creme d'Argent	1	8.5–11.0	3.9–5.0	8–10.5	3.6–4.8
Dutch	6	3.5–5.5	1.6–2.5	3.5–5.5	1.6–2.5
English Spot	7	5–8	2.3–3.6	5–8	2.3–3.6
Flemish Giant	7	13 or over	5.9	12 or over	5.4
Florida White	1	4–6	1.8–2.7	4–6	1.8–2.7
Harlequin	2	6–8	2.7–3.6	6–8	2.7–3.6
Havana	2	5–7	2.3–3.2	5–7	2.3–3.2
Himalayan	2	2.5–4.5	1.1–2.0	2.5–4.5	1.1–2.0
Lilac	1	6–9	2.7–4.1	5.5–8.5	2.5–3.9
Lop (English)	2	10 or over	4.5	9 or over	4.1
Lop (French)	2	10 or over	4.5	9 or over	4.1
Netherland Dwarf	4	2.5 or less	1.1	2.5 or less	1.1
New Zealand	3	10–12	4.5–5.4	9–11	4.1–5.0
Palomino	2	9–11	4.1–5.0	8–10	3.6–4.5
Polish	4	3.5 or less	1.6	3.5 or less	1.6
Rex	13	8 or over	3.6	7 or over	3.2
Rhinelander	1	7.5–9.5	3.4–4.3	7–9	3.2–4.1
Sable	1	8 or over	3.6	7 or over	3.2
Satin	9	9–11	4.1–5.0	8.5–10.5	3.9–4.8
Siamese Sable	1	5–8	2.3–3.6	5–8	2.3–3.6
Silver	3	4–7	1.8–3.2	4–7	1.8–3.2
Silver Fox	2	10–12	4.5–5.4	9–11	4.1–5.0
Silver Marten	4	7.5–9.5	3.4–4.3	6.5–8.5	2.9–3.9
Tan	4	4–6	1.8–2.7	4–5.5	1.8–2.5

Source: Standard of Perfection, American Rabbit Breeders Association, 1976–1980.

blue and should possess good color depth. The American breed is both a fancy and a meat type rabbit. The White was created here from animals which appeared as mutations of the American Blue. The body type is mandolin with medium bone size. The fur is medium length and is considered a commercial fur.

ANGORA

The Angora (Fig. 2.1) is classed as a wool-producing rabbit whereas all other breeds are classed as fur producers as far as the pelt is concerned. It is one of the oldest breeds known and is be-

Fig. 2.1. Angora. (Photo courtesy U.S. Department of Agriculture.)

lieved to have been found originally in Asia Minor and Russia. The name is supposedly adopted from the town of Angora, now Ankara, Turkey. Two breeds are recognized: French and English. The French Angora originated in Turkey and preceded the English variety. For many years French peasants plucked the wool, spun it into strands with hand looms, and knitted the product into finished garments. The wool is coarse with an ideal length of 2-3/4 inches. The French Angora has a longer and narrower head, a longer body, and heavier bone than the English; it is not heavily furnished like the English.

The English Angora was developed from the French commercial type primarily as an exhibition animal. The wool is silky, and the body is compact and cobby with medium bone structure. The head has heavy bangs of hair, side trimmings, and heavily tasseled ears, giving the rabbit the appearance of a round ball of fluff. Fur of the French and English Angoras may be white or colored.

BELGIAN HARE

Although this animal is called a hare, it is actually a rabbit, said to have originated in Belgium. English breeders, however, are given credit for the selected breeding which created the "perfect" Belgian Hare. This rabbit, with its long sleek body, is considered the "racehorse" of the rabbit family. The body is carried well off the ground in contrast to most breeds. The fur is a rich red with a tan or chestnut shade, and the ears are laced with a brilliant black. The fur lies close to the body and has a hard texture. The Belgian Hare is a fancy rabbit which was raised in large numbers in the early 1900s. At present only a few breeders raise this rabbit.

BEVERN

This breed originated in the latter part of the nineteenth century in the town of Bevern in Belgium. Three varieties are recognized: White, Blue, and Black. The White Bevern has blue eyes rather than albino. The body is of medium length with a broad, meaty back. In the United States, the Bevern is raised as a meat as well as a fancy rabbit.

BLUE VIENNA

This breed was recognized in 1974. It is medium weight with an ideal size of 9 pounds for bucks and 9-1/2 for does. Its body is rather rectangular with no tendency toward the mandolin type.

Outer coat hairs are about 1-1/4 inches long and stand near 90°. The undercoat is soft and dense and about one-half the length of the outer coat. Fur is smooth and lustrous with no flyback. Color is clear, dark blue, extending over the entire length of the body.

CALIFORNIAN

This breed (Fig. 2.2) was developed in California from a Himalayan and Standard Chinchilla cross which produced a Chinchilla-colored, half-breed buck. This male was then bred to a

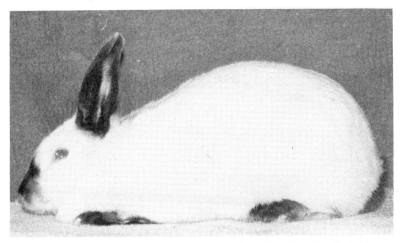

Fig. 2.2. Californian. (Photo courtesy Ann Randles, Ocala, Fl.)

New Zealand White female, and the Californian was produced. It is a white rabbit with black hair on the nose, ears, feet, and tail, but it has albino eyes. The Californian is a commercial meat rabbit and is second to the New Zealand in numbers produced for meat in this country. The body is of medium length with well-developed shoulders and hindquarters.

CHAMPAGNE D'ARGENT

The Champagne (Fig. 2.3) is one of the oldest breeds of rabbit and has been raised since the 1800s. It was originally called the French Silver and was produced in large numbers in the province of Champagne, France. *Argent* is the French word for silver, hence the name. The Champagne is a combination commercial and exhibition animal. It has medium bone, moderate body length, and well-developed shoulders, hindquarters, and back. The color is described as that of old silver with no trace of yellow tinge. The young are solid black when born and begin the change to silver at about four months of age.

Fig. 2.3. Champagne d'Argent. (Photo courtesy Dennis Holcomb, Monclova, Oh.)

CHECKERED GIANT (AMERICAN)

The Checkered Giant (Fig. 2.4) was derived from the Flemish Giant and an unknown white or spotted breed. It was introduced as a distinct breed in Germany and imported into America in 1910. Since that time, American breeders have developed a type that can be easily differentiated from the blocky, heavier boned animals raised in Europe. There are two varieties of the American Checkered Giant: Black and Blue. It is a fancy rabbit in which markings are of prime importance. This breed has a long, arched body which is carried well off the ground.

CHINCHILLA

The three breeds of the Chinchilla rabbit (Standard, American, Giant) share a distinctive color pattern which resembles that of the chinchilla animal. Undercoat hair is dark slate blue at the base, the intermediate portion of the hair shaft is light, and there

Fig. 2.4. Checkered Giant. (Photo courtesy Dennis Holcomb, Monclova, Oh.)

is a narrow black band at the top edge. Each breed has its own standard and crossbreeding is to be discouraged.

A French breeder is credited with producing the present "perfect" Chinchilla, a cross between the Garenre, a blue rabbit, and the Himalayan. It was first exhibited in France in 1913. To improve the fur color and ticking, several other breeds were introduced. In 1917, breeders in England began raising Chinchillas, which were imported into America in 1919. The Standard Chinchilla (Fig. 2.5) has a compact, cobby, medium-length body. The American Chinchilla was originally called the heavyweight Chinchilla and resulted from selective breeding for size from the Standard Chinchilla. The American has a medium-length body and well-filled loin and hips. At maturity it is about 4 pounds heavier than the Standard. The Giant Chinchilla was produced by crossbreeding with the Flemish Giant. This is the only giant breed important in meat production. At maturity, the Giant Chinchilla bucks weigh 12–15 pounds and the does 13–16 pounds.

CINNAMON

The Cinnamon rabbit was recently developed in Montana and was accepted as a breed by the ARBA in 1972. New Zealand White, Californian, Standard Chinchilla, Checkered Giant, and Siamese Satin were used in developing this breed. It is rust or cinnamon with uniform smoke-gray ticking across the back and an orange undercolor. There is a distinct mask on the nose, fading out along the jawline, and there are small, distinct eye circles. Body is of medium length with well-developed shoulders and hindquarters. Mature bucks should weigh 8-1/2–10-1/2 pounds and does 9–11 pounds. The Cinnamon breed was developed primarily as a meat rabbit.

CREME D'ARGENT

The Creme d'Argent originated in France as did its counterpart, the Champagne. The major difference between the two breeds is in fur color. The fur of the Creme is orange-silver; the surface is cream-white with an orange cast while the undercolor is a rich orange. This breed first appeared in the United States in 1924. Although the Creme is similar to the Champagne in body type, it is somewhat smaller.

DUTCH

This breed (Fig. 2.6) originated in Holland. In 1864, it was found in England and now represents one of the most popular fancy breeds in America. The distinctive fur markings are a pure

Fig. 2.5. Standard Chinchilla. (Photo courtesy Dennis Holcomb, Monclova, Oh.)

Fig. 2.6. Dutch. (Photo courtesy Ann Randles, Ocala, Fl.)

genetic factor. Six varieties are presently recognized in the
United States: Chocolate, Black, Blue, Tortoise, Steel-Gray, and
Gray. The Dutch rabbit has a compact and cobby body, and
although it is one of the smaller breeds, its carcass contains a
considerable amount of flesh on a compact frame and there is a
high dressing percentage. This breed is produced primarily as
a fancy animal, but is also used for meat and in the laboratory,
where it is desirable because of its small size. It is second to the
New Zealand White in the number used for research.

Fig. 2.7. English Spot. (Photo courtesy Dennis Holcomb, Monclova,
Oh.)

ENGLISH SPOT

The English Spot (Fig. 2.7) has been bred in England since 1880,
and, although it existed prior to that time, its origin is not known.
It is said to be descended from the old Flemish breeds and sub-
species of white or spotted wild rabbits. There are seven varieties
of the English Spot: Black, Blue, Chocolate, Gold, Gray, Lilac,
and Tortoise. The body is of the racy type, carried well off the
ground. The English Spot is strictly a fancy rabbit. Its markings
make it a very distinctive rabbit, but it is difficult to obtain

specimens having the proper spotted markings. Litters normally contain solid-colored rabbits (selfs) and very lightly marked rabbits (charlies). The usual overall pattern ratio in litters is 50 per cent marked, 25 per cent charlies, and 25 per cent selfs.

FLEMISH GIANT

There are seven varieties of the Flemish Giant: Steel-Gray, Black-Gray, Sandy, Black, Blue, White, and Fawn. Opinions differ as to the origin of this breed. It is undisputed, however, that Flanders (northern Belgium) was the country of its adoption and dissemination throughout Europe before it appeared in America. The Flemish Giant is the largest of the domestic breeds and has a well-proportioned and balanced body.

FLORIDA WHITE

The Florida White rabbit was developed in that state and recognized as a breed about 1966. Dutch, Polish, and New Zealand White rabbits were used in the initial breeding, but genetic proportions of the different breeds are unknown. It was developed as a small albino laboratory rabbit, but so far has not been extensively used for this purpose. Scientists are reluctant to change to another breed for which little biological data are available. Presently it is classified as a small meat and fancy animal. It is cobby and compact, maturing at 4–6 pounds.

HARLEQUIN

This rabbit originated in France and has been raised throughout that country for a number of years. It descended from the Dutch and colored rabbits of English or Checkered classification and was first exhibited in 1887 in Paris. There are two varieties, Harlequin and Magpie, and both are bred in blue, black, chocolate, and lilac. The colors alternate with bands of orange or light orange in the Harlequin and with white in the Magpie. The Harlequin is a fancy rabbit that can be utilized for meat.

HAVANA

The Havana is a small, fancy type rabbit with two varieties: Chocolate and Blue. The Chocolate appeared in a litter of a Dutch-marked doe in 1898 in Holland. These were bred and gained rapid popularity in France, Switzerland, and Germany. Havana rabbits were imported into America in 1916, and the Blue Havana was developed in this country. Its characteristic fur is soft, lustrous, and possesses a good sheen, and it has a well-rounded and compact body. It can be utilized as a small meat rabbit.

HIMALAYAN

The Himalayan rabbit has inhabited the countries north and south of the Himalayan mountains for many years. It is also found in great numbers in China and Russia and probably originated in the East. The Himalayan characteristics are distinctive: its trim body is covered with short, white fur, and its nose, ears, feet, and tail are black. A small rabbit, it weighs 2-1/2–4-1/2 pounds at maturity and is considered strictly a fancy rabbit in the United States.

LILAC

The Lilac originated as a sport from the Havana. Hair coats of various shades were obtained by crossing the Havana with a blue rabbit and interbreeding the young. The ideal color is light lilac, generally referred to as pinky-dove. The Lilac is an ideal small meat rabbit. It has a small, compact body frame that carries considerable flesh, and the loss in dressing is low.

LOP

Origin of the Lop rabbit has not been documented. It is thought to have appeared first in North Africa and then to have spread to France, Belgium, and the Netherlands. There is evidence of British origin, and it is the oldest of the fancy varieties there. In

England, breeders vied with one another to produce animals with outstanding ear lengths. They gradually increased the size until ears measuring 24 inches from tip to tip became quite common. Two breeds of the Lop rabbit are recognized in the United States: English and French. Breeders of the English type emphasize the development of very long, wide ears. The body is of medium length. The French Lop differs from the English in having a massive, thick-set body. Both breeds allow self or broken color, the broken colors being any other color in conjunction with white.

NETHERLAND DWARF

The Netherland Dwarf is thought to have originated in Holland as a cross between the Polish rabbit and a small wild rabbit. The Dwarf was popular for many years before British fanciers brought it to England around 1948. In America, the rabbit was accepted as a breed by the ARBA in 1969. It has become quite popular in this country, and, as a result, there have been a number of importations. The Dwarf is the smallest of all domestic breeds, but has the greatest variety of color and coat patterns. It is a fancy breed and is sold in large numbers for pets because of its small size. Mature weight should not be over 2-1/2 pounds for the male or female. There are many color pattern variations: there are selfs with five subcolors, shaded with three subcolors, an Agouti pattern with five, a tan pattern with five subcolors, and other varieties with five subcolors. Fur texture should be dense with good flyback. The general body type is short, compact, and cobby, with wide shoulders.

NEW ZEALAND

This breed is one of the best known and is most extensively produced in this country for meat and as a laboratory animal. There are three varieties—White, Red, and Black—which are unrelated genetically. The first of the New Zealands produced was the red variety which is commonly believed to have been the result of a cross between a Belgian Hare and a white rabbit. Red New Zealands appeared simultaneously in California and Indiana around 1912. The White (Fig. 2.8) was the result of crosses among a number of breeds including Flemish, American Whites, and Angoras. Several strains of White New Zealands originated in different parts of this country from various crosses. The White was accepted as a breed by the ARBA in the mid-1920s. The Black variety appeared much later from various crosses including the Giant Chinchilla; it was developed through the efforts of breeders in California and in the eastern United States.

Fig. 2.8. New Zealand White. (Photo courtesy Ann Randles, Ocala, Fl.)

The New Zealand rabbit is of medium body length, has well-rounded hips and well-filled loin and ribs. An animal typical of the breed must exemplify meat producing qualities.

PALOMINO

The Palomino was developed in the state of Washington from a combination of breeds crossed to produce a true breeding animal of distinctive colors. It was created to be a meat-producer and to have an attractive appearance. Of the two varieties, Golden and Lynx, fur of the former is a light golden shade with cream white undercolor. The Lynx coat has a silver sheen over a bright orange intermediate color above a base color and is lightly and evenly ticked with lilac.

POLISH

The date and place of origin of this breed are not known and many doubt a Polish origin. It was bred for many years in Europe, and as early as 1884 it was being shown in England. Some of its ancestors appeared as albino forms of Dutch and were utilized in establishing the breed. The four varieties are: Black, Chocolate, Blue-eyed White, and Ruby-eyed White. The Polish is a fancy rabbit with a small and compact body, well-rounded hips, and short, fine, dense fur. At maturity bucks and does weigh 3-1/2 pounds or less.

REX

The Rex rabbit is differentiated from other breeds by its coat. The main characteristic—short coat with no conspicuous guard hairs—is now a fixed, constant genetic factor. Guard hairs are present, but they remain the same length as the undercoat instead of developing into the normal prominent guard hairs common to other breeds. Rex fur is the most valuable type of rabbit fur. This rabbit is a well-proportioned animal exemplifying meat qualities. It has a medium body length and medium bone.

RHINELANDER

The Rhinelander was recognized as a breed in 1974. It is smaller than the medium-weight breeds with an ideal of 8 pounds for bucks and 8-1/2 for does. Body type is rounded without heaviness in the shoulders or hindquarters. The short, dense fur has a silky texture, short guard hairs, and typical flyback; it is bright golden-orange with distinct black spots.

SABLE

Two breeds of Sable rabbits are recognized in the United States. One is known simply as the Sable and the other as the Siamese Sable. Both were developed as sports from the Chinchilla or as the result of Chinchilla crosses. The Sable, the darker of the two, has at times been crossed with the Chocolate Havana to obtain a deeper sepia color. The body type of both Sable breeds is similar, being of medium length and bone, but the Siamese breed at maturity weighs less than the Sable (Table 2.1).

SATIN

This rabbit (Fig. 2.9) is differentiated from normal-furred rabbits by its coat. The satin mutation was first observed in America in the mid-1930s in litters of Chocolate Havanas. The mutation gives the guard hairs the appearance of satin and has resulted in a number of breeds having a "satin" counterpart.

Nine varieties are presently known: Black, Blue, Californian, Chinchilla, Chocolate, Copper, Red, Siamese, and White. All varieties of Satin have a fur color comparable to that of the normal fur breeds with the exception of the Copper and Siamese.

SILVER

Silver Gray rabbits existed many years ago in India. It is believed that Portuguese sailors brought them to Europe in the seventeenth century. Three varieties of the Silver rabbit are recognized: Brown, Fawn, and Gray. The Brown was perfected in England by crossing the original Fawn with the Belgian. The Fawn is supposed to have come from a Creme d'Argent. Lighter-colored Browns, however, when crossed with Grays will also produce the Fawn color. Gray is the most popular color.

The Silver is a fancy rabbit with a hair coat perfected by the fancier so that there is uniform silvering and ticking of the entire body, ears, and feet.

SILVER FOX

This breed, larger than the Silver, is thought to have resulted from a cross between a Checkered Giant and a Silver. It was accepted as a breed in the United States in 1925. There are two varieties: Blue and Black. Fur of the former is medium blue with slate gray undercolor; the black is jet black with a dark slate gray undercolor. A distinctive characteristic of both varieties is a long, evenly silvered coat resembling fox fur; flyback in the coat is not desirable. The body is of medium length and medium bone.

SILVER MARTEN

This breed (Fig. 2.10) is known in England as the Silver Fox and exists as Blue, Black, Chocolate, and Sable varieties. It was developed as a sport from the Chinchilla and has a medium-length

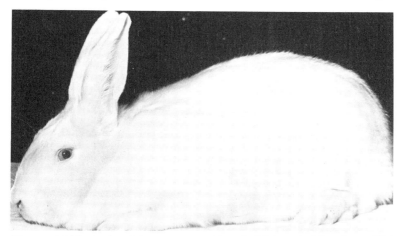

Fig. 2.9. White Satin. (Photo courtesy Dennis Holcomb, Monclova, Oh.)

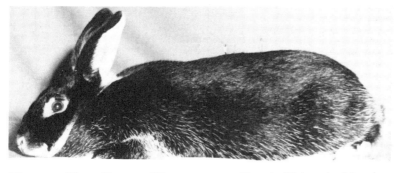

Fig. 2.10. Silver Marten. (Photo courtesy Dennis Holcomb, Monclova, Oh.)

body with well-developed hindquarters and shoulders. The fur is about 1 inch long and is interspersed with white-tipped guard hairs evenly distributed over the body, sides, and hips. It is a fancy breed, the culls of which can be sold as small fryers.

TAN

There are four varieties of the Tan breed: Black, Blue, Chocolate, and Lilac. The original Black and Tan rabbits were sports from the mating in England of a wild rabbit with a Dutch. It was first shown in France in 1894 and remains a popular fancy breed there. Markings of the Tan rabbit are a stable genetic feature. The body color is solid with the tan markings confined to a triangle at the nape of the neck, inner part of the front and hind legs, toes, chest, underside of the body, flanks, and underside of the tail.

SAN JUAN

The San Juan rabbit is not recognized as a domestic breed, but it is gaining attention as a laboratory animal (Thomsen and Evans, 1964). It is believed to have originated from Belgian Hares imported about 1900 with some Black Flemish and New Zealand breeding introduced later. This rabbit exists in rather large numbers in the wild state on the island of San Juan near the coast of Washington State. It is usually brown with shadings of light to dark and is similar in size to the Dutch. Adult females in the laboratory or domesticated state weigh about 5-1/2 pounds and males 4-3/4; those in the wild state are smaller. The San Juan adapts quite well to laboratory and domestic conditions.

BREED SELECTION

With the many breeds of domestic rabbits and with the many different characteristics which make them suitable for different purposes, choosing a breed becomes a matter of importance. The beginning producer must carefully select the breed or breeds to be raised, and occasionally the established breeder may have to reevaluate his breeds and purposes. These choices should be made on the basis of several important considerations: purposes or objectives in raising rabbits, markets available for different breeds, availability of good breeding stock, facilities (housing) available, previous experience, and personal preference.

The purpose—meat production, laboratory animals, fancy animals, or pets—should play a major role in the decision concerning a breed. Rabbits raised for meat should be one of the medium-weight breeds such as the New Zealand or Californian. Fryer rabbits of these breeds produce the size carcass to which the meat market has become accustomed. Other breeds may be marketed for meat, but the New Zealand and Californian are the most widely used.

If the objective is to supply the laboratory animal market, the New Zealand White should be the first choice, followed by the Dutch. Research workers have used the New Zealand White for many years, and the biological data accumulated plus the experience with this breed make it likely that it will continue to be the one most widely used. More than one-half of all rabbits used in research are New Zealand White.

Personal preference for a breed is most often related to fancy breeds and can be an important factor in selection when other guidelines are not applicable. Considering the production for meat only, several breeds are about equally useful, and personal preference may be a logical factor in selection. Except for these situations, however, personal preference should not play a major role in the decision; the guidelines relating to markets, availability of quality breeding stock, and purpose of production are more important.

It should be emphasized that rabbit production need not be limited to only one purpose and one breed, but the average producer should not attempt to raise rabbits for all purposes. Frequently, however, several objectives and several breeds will provide expanded markets. If a producer normally markets laboratory rabbits but the demand decreases, the rabbits may be diverted to the meat market.

Rabbits to be produced for pets are best selected from the smaller breeds and those which are colored. These breeds do not necessarily make better pets, but the small size and colored hair coat are preferred.

When rabbits are to be raised as a hobby only, then the choice of breed can be made largely on the basis of personal preference. If, however, the producer wishes to sell breeding stock, the potential demand for the breed should be a guide in selection. The breeds desirable for pets and fancy animals may vary in different parts of the country. Preferences in a certain locality should be studied so that better market outlets may be sought.

Availability of good quality breeding stock should also be a selection factor. If high quality foundation breeding animals of a particular breed are not available, it may be best to select another breed or to delay purchase until suitable animals can be found. An attempt to establish a breeding herd with inferior representatives of the breed is unwise.

The size of available housing facilities may play a small part in the selection of breeds. When space for housing is limited, the use of a small breed will permit the handling of a larger number of rabbits. Since small rabbits are preferable for sale as pets, one or more of these breeds may well be the desirable selection under these conditions. Lower feed costs for small rabbits may also be a factor in breed selection. It is best to begin with one or perhaps two breeds and expand, if desirable, as experience and markets develop. Considerable time, effort, and experience are required to breed quality animals, and the attempt by a beginner to maintain several breeds is likely to be rewarded with poor quality animals.

SOURCES AND PURCHASE OF BREEDING STOCK

Once the choice of a breed or breeds has been made, suitable breeding or foundation stock must be procured. Frequently, the rabbits may be purchased from a local breeder and it is well to know his reputation and the quality of animals that he has maintained over a period of time. Classified ads in rabbit magazines and in periodicals issued by local and state rabbit organizations usually carry listings of animals available. The ARBA maintains a list of members from whom animals may usually be purchased. If rabbits are to be bought from a breeder who is selling his entire colony, the reasons for the sale should be determined. Frequently, good quality rabbits may be obtained in this way; on the other hand, the owner may be disposing of them because they are of poor quality or are poor producers.

In actually choosing the animals to be foundation breeders, the rabbits, their production records and quality, and the reputation of the breeder should be evaluated. Individual rabbits of both sexes should be typical of the breed in size, color markings, and other characteristics. They should be healthy, vigorous, alert, have a sleek hair coat, and possess characteristics of the breed. The appearance of an animal, however, does not indicate its ability to reproduce. If the rabbits are adult and have produced litters, the production records (number of litters and number of young per litter) should be studied. If the rabbits are young and have not produced litters, then production records of their ancestors should be examined if possible.

REFERENCES

American Rabbit Breeders Association. 1976. *Standard of Perfection.* American Rabbit Breeders Association: Bloomington, Illinois.

Arrington, L. R. 1967. The Florida White rabbit. Small Stock Magazine 51: 7.

Cahalane, V. H. 1961. *Mammals of North America.* Macmillan Co.: New York.

Denenberg, V. H., M. X. Zarrow, and S. Ross. 1969. The behavior of rabbits. In *The Behavior of Domestic Animals.* 2d ed., ed. E. S. E. Hafez. Williams and Wilkins: Baltimore, Maryland.

Eveleigh, J. R., and R. G. Mardell. 1968. The Dutch rabbit. J. Inst. Anim. Tech. 19: 111–20.

Grossman, K. E. 1967. Behavioral differences between rabbits and cats. J. Genet. Psych. 111: 171.

Heath, E. 1972. Sexual and related territorial behavior in the laboratory rabbit (*Oryctolagus cuniculus*). Lab. Anim. Sci. 22: 684–91.

Lockley, R. M. 1966. *The Private Life of the Rabbit*. October House: New York.

Martin, C. E. 1970. Effects of anxiety on rabbits. (Text in Spanish.) Ceres 35: 25.

Myers, K., and R. Mykytowycz. 1958. Social behavior in the wild rabbit. Nature 181: 1515–16.

Nachtsheim, H. 1949. *Vom Wildtier Zum Haustier*. Parey: Berlin.

Stodart, E., and K. Myers. 1964. A comparison of behavior, reproduction and mortality of wild and domestic rabbits in confined populations. csiro Wildlife Res. 9: 144–59.

Thomsen, J. J., and C. A. Evans. 1964. The feral San Juan rabbit as a potential useful laboratory animal. Lab. Anim. Care 14: 155–60.

Walker, E. P. 1964. *Mammals of the World*. The Johns Hopkins Press: Baltimore, Maryland.

Zeuner, F. E. 1963. *A History of Domesticated Animals*. Hutchinson and Co.: London.

3. BIOLOGY OF THE RABBIT

Biological characteristics of the rabbit, in terms of gross anatomy and physiology, are similar to those of other domestic animals. Many texts and manuals (Frandson, 1965; Swenson, 1970; McLaughlin, 1970) provide basic information on mammalian anatomy and physiology applicable to the rabbit. The purpose of this chapter is to report specific biological data and to describe those features peculiar to the rabbit. Some aspects of rabbit biology have been included in the previous chapter, and additional characteristics relating to reproduction, nutrition, genetics, and disease will be included in subsequent sections.

Tabular data for the more common biological and physiological characteristics are presented in Table 3.1. Additional information may be reviewed in the data books and other references cited at the end of the chapter. Since rabbits are used extensively in medical and biological research, many of these values pertaining to the species have been determined. The skeletal system of the rabbit is illustrated in Figure 3.1, and blood values are included in Table 3.1.

GROSS BODY COMPOSITION

The composition of the rabbit body in terms of the major components and in comparison to certain other species is indicated in Table 3.2. These values represent the composition of the whole body, less contents of the digestive tract, and should not be confused with data in Table 10.2, indicating the edible portion of the carcass. The percentage composition varies under

39

TABLE 3.1. Basic Biological and Physiological Data[a]

	Average	Range[b]
Mature weight		
lbs		
Male	10	9–11
Female	11	10–12
kg		
Male	4.5	4.1–5.0
Female	5.0	4.5–5.5
Birth weight		
oz	2.35	
g	64	
Eyes open, days	10	
Begins solid feed, days	21	18–23
Litter size	8	1–13
Life span, years	5	13 max.
Reproductive life, years	2.5	
Daily feed		
oz	7	6–9
g	200	160–250
Daily water, ml/kg, body wt/day	120	60–250
Daily urine, ml/kg, body wt/day	65	50–75
Body temperature, °F	102.1	101.0–103.2
Respiratory rate	46	36–56
Heart rate	205	123–304
Blood volume, ml/100 g	5.4	4.5–8.1
Blood pressure		
Systolic	110	95–130
Diastolic	80	60–90
Hemoglobin, g/100 ml	11.9	8–15
Hematocrit	41.5	33–50
Erythrocytes, millions/cu mm	5.4	4.5–7.0
Sedimentation rate, mm/hr	2	1–3
Leucocytes, thousands/cu mm		
Total	8.9	5.2–12
Neutrophils	4.1	2.5–6.0
Eosinophils	0.18	0.0–0.4
Basophils	0.45	0.15–0.75
Lymphocytes	3.5	2.0–5.6
Monocytes	0.72	0.3–1.3
Platelets, thousands/cu mm	533	170–1120
Blood pH	7.35	7.21–7.57

a. Values for weight and feed for adult New Zealand White breed.
b. Range of normal values or range of values reported.

certain conditions. Water decreases with age, being very high in the embryo; at birth, water content is about 85 per cent and in the adult about 69 per cent. The amount of fat varies with the condition of the animal. It is normally low in young animals and increases with age up to about 8 per cent in the adult rabbit. Protein and ash or mineral matter remain rather constant in the animal on a dry matter basis.

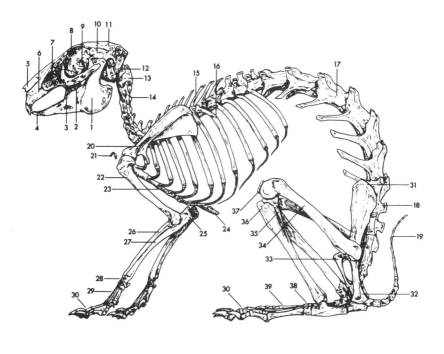

1. Mandible	14. Cervical vertebra (7)	27. Ulna
2. Molar	15. Thoracic vertebra (12)	28. Carpals
3. Premolar	16. Ribs (12)	29. Metacarpals
4. Incisor	17. Lumbar vertebra (7)	30. Phalanges
5. Nasal	18. Sacral vertebra (4)	31. Ilium
6. Premaxilla	19. Caudal vertebra (16)	32. Ischium
7. Maxilla	20. Scapula	33. Pubis
8. Frontal	21. Clavicle	34. Femur
9. Optic foramen	22. Humerus	35. Fibula
10. Squamosal	23. Sternum	36. Tibia
11. Parietal	24. Xiphoid process	37. Patella
12. Atlas	25. Olecranon process	38. Tarsals
13. Axis	26. Radius	39. Metatarsals

Fig. 3.1. Rabbit skeleton. (Photo copyright © 1968 by the Carolina Biological Supply Company, Burlington, N.C.)

GROWTH

Newborn rabbits grow rapidly and more than double the birth weight by 1 week if the doe is lactating normally. At 4 weeks, when growth is still dependent upon the mother's milk, the weight is approximately 12 per cent of the adult weight. By 8 weeks the weight approaches 40 per cent of the mature weight. Data in Figure 3.2 represent weights of New Zealand White rabbits at different ages. Females are larger than males in most breeds and weights shown after 8 weeks reflect this. In view of the wide range in size and other characteristics of different breeds, it must be expected that growth rates would be slightly

TABLE 3.2. APPROXIMATE PERCENTAGE COMPOSITION OF THE ANIMAL BODY[a]

Animal	Water	Protein	Fat	Ash
Rabbit				
Newborn[b]	85	11	2	
Adult	69	18	8	4.8
Hen	56	21	19	3.2
Pig	49	12	36	2.6
Man	59	18	18	4.3

a. Less contents of the digestive tract. SOURCE: *Animal Nutrition* by Maynard and Loosli, McGraw-Hill, New York.
b. Widdowson, 1950.

different. Even within breeds, there are small differences in growth of the different strains. Milk production of the doe and number of young per litter have a major effect on early growth. At 6 weeks of age, when most of the weight is dependent upon milk consumed, the weight of individual young in a litter of 8 or 9 will be about 80–85 per cent of the weight of young in a litter of 4.

DIGESTIVE SYSTEM

The rabbit has been referred to as a pseudoruminant, but the digestive system (Fig. 3.3) does not function like that of the ruminant, and the alimentary tract of the rabbit is characteristic of monogastric animals. The term "pseudoruminant" has been applied to the rabbit because it consumes and recycles a portion of its fecal matter. In this process, known as coprophagy (see below), certain nutrients synthesized in the lower intestinal tract are made available to the rabbit.

The stomach is divided into three regions: the cardiac portion near the esophagus, the fundus or sac-like portion to the left of

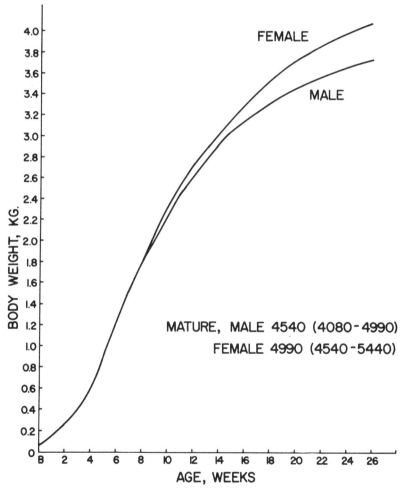

Fig. 3.2. Growth rate of New Zealand White rabbits.

the cardiac region, and the pyloric region near the small intestine. Stomach volume is about 36 per cent of the total volume of the intestinal tract. The pH in the stomach is about 1.9. The duodenal portion of the small intestine with ducts for the digestive secretions is rather long. Volume of the small intestine

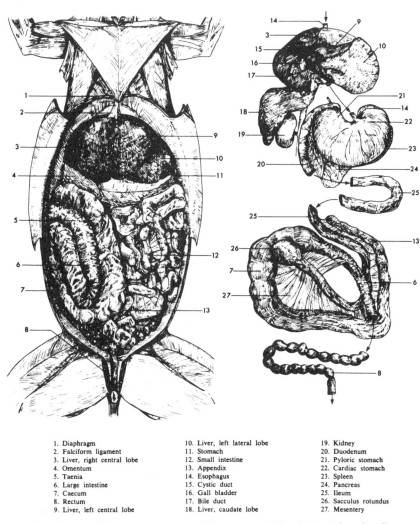

1. Diaphragm	10. Liver, left lateral lobe	19. Kidney
2. Falciform ligament	11. Stomach	20. Duodenum
3. Liver, right central lobe	12. Small intestine	21. Pyloric stomach
4. Omentum	13. Appendix	22. Cardiac stomach
5. Taenia	14. Esophagus	23. Spleen
6. Large intestine	15. Cystic duct	24. Pancreas
7. Caecum	16. Gall bladder	25. Ileum
8. Rectum	17. Bile duct	26. Sacculus rotundus
9. Liver, left central lobe	18. Liver, caudate lobe	27. Mesentery

Fig. 3.3. Rabbit digestive system. (Photo copyright © 1969 by the Carolina Biological Supply Company, Burlington, N.C.)

represents 10 per cent of the total tract. The cecum or blind pouch joins the small intestine at its terminus and at the first segment of the colon. It is connected to the intestine only at the entrance. This large, coiled cecum is the largest segment of the tract, making up about 42 per cent of the total volume.

Digestion of food nutrients takes place under the influence of enzymes as is characteristic of other monogastric animals. Significant synthesis of some of the B-vitamins and possibly some amino acids takes place in the lower intestinal tract, primarily in the cecum and large intestine, by microbial action. The benefits of this synthesis are made available to the rabbit through its practice of coprophagy. Since the rabbit is herbivorous, consuming the vegetative portion of plants as well as the seed, it has been assumed that this animal can digest and utilize significant amounts of crude fiber. Actually, the rabbit digests relatively small amounts of fiber, possibly less than 20 per cent or about one-half the amount digested by the guinea pig and the horse. The fiber digestion which does occur, however, apparently does not take place in the cecum. When the cecum is removed, there is little or no change in the amount of the crude fiber digested by the rabbit, although there is a decrease in vitamin synthesis (De Oms and Leffel, 1972).

Microorganisms of the intestinal tract have not been studied extensively, but some research indicates unusual microflora characteristics (Smith, 1965). *Escherichia coli, Clostridium, Lactobacillus,* and yeasts are normally absent. Bacteroids are present in the large intestine and probably comprise the primary flora in adult animals.

COPROPHAGY

Coprophagy refers to the act of eating feces and is a normal practice of some animals. They may consume a portion of their own fecal excreta or that of others. Animals that practice coprophagy are able to obtain certain nutrients, especially water-soluble vitamins, which have been synthesized by microorganisms living in the intestinal tract. Rabbits consume a portion of their feces in a manner which is different from other animals. They excrete two types of fecal matter: the dry, hard, rounded pellets normally observed, and a moist, jelly-like material referred to as the soft or night feces. It is the latter type that the rabbit consumes, collecting it directly from the anus as it is excreted. The act of eating these feces is seldom observed, and it was formerly thought to occur only at night. To collect this fecal matter, it is necessary to collar the rabbit or restrain it in some way. The soft pellets are observed whole in the fundus portion of the stomach, so it is believed they are swallowed whole, although the rabbit appears to be chewing them when ingesting.

Coprophagy in the rabbit has been referred to occasionally as "pseudorumination." It aids in digestion, but it does not correspond to the rumination process characteristic of cattle, sheep, and other ruminants. The practice starts shortly after the rabbit begins to eat solid feed, at 3–4 weeks of age. It has been known since 1882 (Morot, 1882), but apparently its significance has not been recognized for it has been "re-discovered" several times. The eating of feces occurs in domestic and wild rabbits, but it does not occur in germ-free rabbits.

It is thought that the soft feces form in the cecum and rapidly pass out through the large intestine with little time for a change in consistency. They appear as clusters, but each pellet is surrounded by a membrane. A comparison of the composition of dry and soft feces is shown in Table 3.3. Soft feces contain more moisture than regular feces as may be expected from the moist, mucus-like appearance of the pellet. Of particular importance, however, is the protein and vitamin content. Microorganisms living in the cecum and lower intestinal tract are able to synthesize certain vitamins and these are made available to the rabbit through consumption of the fecal matter. It has been determined from a study of the effects of coprophagy on excretion of B-vitamins that coprophagy provides the rabbit with about 83 per cent more niacin, 100 per cent more riboflavin, 165 per cent more pantothenic acid, and 42 per cent more vitamin B_{12} than would be available if the soft feces were not consumed (Kulwich et al., 1953). If the cecum is removed, coprophagy is not prac-

ticed, but both types of feces are still excreted. In the cececto-
mized rabbit, the soft feces are not excreted in the grape-like
clusters characteristic of normal night feces and the gelatinous-
like coating is absent. Protein content of the soft feces of cecec-
tomized rabbits is less than in normal rabbits (Herndon and
Hove, 1955).

The practice of coprophagy by rabbits is perfectly normal.
It is an advantage in digestion and in supplying additional B-
vitamins, but there is no means of increasing this activity in an
effort to improve efficiency. It is possible that different types of

TABLE 3.3. COMPARISON OF THE COMPOSITION OF SOFT FECES
AND DRY FECES OF THE RABBIT

	Diet Fed	Soft Feces	Dry Feces
Dry matter, g		6.9	9.8
Crude protein, %	17.5	37.4	18.7
Fat, %	9.1	3.5	4.3
Ash, %	9.9	13.1	13.2
Cellulose, %	21.0	27.2	46.6
Other carbohydrates, %	38.1	11.3	4.9
Niacin, $\mu g/g$		139.1	39.7
Riboflavin, $\mu g/g$		30.2	9.4
Pantothenic acid, $\mu g/g$		51.6	8.4
Vitamin B_{12}, $\mu g/g$		2.9	0.9

SOURCES: Major nutrients, dry matter basis, from Thacker and Brandt,
1955; vitamin data from Kulwich, Struglia, and Pearson, 1953.

feeds or other factors may affect the degree of coprophagy, but
this has not been established.

GALL BLADDER

Although the gall bladder is a functional structure in most common mammals except the rat and is usually present in the rabbit,
a small number of otherwise normal domestic rabbits do not
possess this organ (Sawin and Crary, 1951; Wallace and Arrington, 1968). About 10 per cent of the animals in a closed
colony of Dutch rabbits in the authors' laboratory did not have

the gall bladder; the bile duct was present and bile was apparently delivered directly into the intestinal tract. Dye injected into the bile duct moved freely into the liver. In approximately 2–3 per cent of additional animals studied, the gall bladders were very small and some were shaped abnormally. The rabbits which had no gall bladder or had an abnormally small gall bladder were otherwise normal and were equal in size to their litter mates.

HYPNOSIS

A hypnotic or somnolent state resembling hypnosis can be induced readily in the rabbit. When properly carried out and monitored it can be used instead of anesthesia as an effective restraint and method of immobilization for several procedures. It can be practiced on rabbits of different ages, and little training or experience is required.

The rabbit is placed on its back, and procedures to aid in relaxation are administered. The animal must remain completely inverted and some support (a V-shaped trough or other device) to maintain this position is helpful. Gentle stroking of the chest and abdomen in the direction of the hair, rubbing the sides of the head in the temple area with slight pressure, and using a low monotone voice or noise appear to help induce the hypnosis. Recovery is immediate when the rabbit is allowed to return to a normal standing or sitting position.

Effectiveness of the hypnosis is indicated by deep breathing, partial closing of the eyes, and a fixed lateral stare. Sudden noises or movement may arouse the rabbit from the trance. If recovery appears to occur, the state may be reinduced using the some procedure. When properly carried out, the hypnotic state is sufficient for injection, heart puncture, and other procedures which may otherwise require anesthesia. The hypnotic state combined with physical restraint makes minor surgery and other procedures possible without use of anesthesia. Advantages of this method are that little time and equipment are required, and recovery is rapid without the side effects, expense, and slow recovery time characteristic of anesthetic drugs. Among the disadvantages are the facts that the hypnotic state may be short lasting and stimuli such as noise may arouse the animal.

REFERENCES

Altman, P. L., and D. S. Dittmer, eds. Vol. 1, 1972, Vol. 2, 1973, Vol. 3, 1974. *Biology Data Book*. Federation of American Societies for Experimental Biology: Washington, D.C.

Badawy, A. M., A. S. El-Bashary, and Z. R. Abo-El-Ezz. 1972. The changing composition of the digesta along the alimentary tract of the rabbit. Alexandria J. Agr. Res. 20: 37–42.

Burns, K. F., and C. W. deLannoy. 1966. Compendium of normal blood values of laboratory animals with indication of variations. 1. Random sexed population of small animals. Toxicol. App. Pharmacol. 8: 429–37.

Buser, P., and G. Viala. 1972. Comments on the akinesis induced in animals and its mechanism. Rev. Pathol. Comp. Med. Exp. 72: 205–12.

Cizek, L. J. 1961. Relationship between food and water ingestion in the rabbit. Am. J. Physiol. 201: 557–66.

Cools, A., and C. Jeuniaux. 1961. Fermentation of cellulose and absorption of volatile fatty acids in the cecum of the rabbit. Arch. Internat. Physiol. 69: 1–8.

Davies, J. S., E. M. Widdowson, and R. A. McCance. 1964. The intake of milk and the retention of its constituents while the newborn doubles its weight. Brit. J. Nutr. 18: 385–92.

DeOms, G. C., and E. C. Leffel. 1972. Effect of cecectomy on digestive processes in the rabbit. J. Anim. Sci. 35: 215 (Abs.).

Dittmer, D. S., ed. 1961. *Blood and Other Body Fluids*. Federation of American Societies for Experimental Biology: Washington, D.C.

Eden, A. 1940. Coprophagy in the rabbit. Nature (London) 145: 36–37.

Eden, A. 1940. Coprophagy in the rabbit. Origin of the night feces. Nature (London) 145: 628–32.

Fioramonti, J., and Y. Ruckebusch. 1974. Caecal motility in the rabbit. 1. Motility patterns. (Text in French, English summary.) Ann. Rech. Vet. 5: 1–13.

Fioramonti, J., and Y. Ruckebusch. 1974. Caecal motility in the rabbit. 2. Changes due to feeding patterns. (Text in French, English summary.) Ann. Rech. Vet. 5: 201–12.

Fox, R. R., G. Schlager, and C. W. Laird. 1969. Blood pressure in thirteen strains of rabbits. J. Hered. 60: 312–14.

Frandson, R. D. 1965. *Anatomy and Physiology of Farm Animals*. Lea and Febiger: Philadelphia, Pennsylvania.

Griffiths, M., and D. Davies. 1963. The role of the soft pellets in the production of lactic acid in the rabbit stomach. J. Nutr. 80: 171–80.

Gruber, R. P., and J. J. Amoto. 1970. Hypnosis for rabbit surgery. Lab. Anim. Care 20: 741–42.

Herndon, J. F., and E. L. Hove. 1955. Surgical removal of the cecum and its effect on digestion and growth in rabbits. J. Nutr. 57: 261–70.

Hiner, R. L. 1962. Physical composition of fryer rabbits of prime, choice and commercial grades. CA–44–37, U.S. Department of Agriculture: Washington, D.C.

Jaeger, R., and G. Donnhauser. 1973. Blood volume of rabbits during pregnancy and lactation. (Text in German, English summary.) Z. Tierzucht Zuchtungsbiol. 89: 242–50.

Jelenko, C., A. P. Anderson, T. H. Scott, Jr., and M. L. Wheeler. 1971. Organ weights and water consumption of the New Zealand albino rabbit (*O. cuniculus*). Am. J. Vet. Res. 32: 1637–39.

Krull, W. 1943. Coprophagy in the wild rabbit, *Sylvilagus nuttallii grangeri*. Vet. Med. 38: 72.

Kulwich, R., L. Struglia, and P. B. Pearson. 1953. The effects of co-phrophagy on the excretion of B-vitamins by the rabbit. J. Nutr. 49: 639–45.

Levine, C. J., W. Mann, H. C. Hodge, I. Ariel, and O. DuPont. 1941. Distribution of body weight in the organs and tissues of the rabbit. Proc. Soc. Exp. Biol. Med. 47: 318–21.

Little, R. A. 1970. Changes in blood volume of the rabbit with age. J. Physiol. 208: 485–97.

McLaughlin, C. A. 1970. *Laboratory Anatomy of the Rabbit*. Wm. C. Brown Co.: Dubuque, Iowa.

Madsen, H. 1939. Does the rabbit chew its cud? Nature (London) 143: 981–82.

Morot, C. 1882. Des pelotes stomacal des leporides. Mem. Soc. Centr. Med. Vet. 12, Ser. 1.

Nichelmann, M., L. Lyhs, H. Rohling, and M. Rott. 1973. Body temperature of the rabbit. (Text in German, English summary.) Arch. Exp. Veterinarmed. 27: 775–82.

Purvis, G. M., and M. M. Sewell. 1973. Leucocyte counts in normal young rabbits. Brit. Vet. J. 129: 47–51.

Rapson, N. S., and T. C. Jones. 1964. Restraint of rabbits by hypnosis. Lab. Anim. Care 14: 131–33.

Rott, M., M. Nichelmann, H. Rohling, and L. Lyhs. 1973. Body temperature of the rabbit. 1. Rectal temperature. (Text in German, English summary.) Arch. Exp. Veterinarmed. 27: 769–74.

Sawin, P. B., and D. D. Crary. 1951. Morphogenetic studies of the rabbit. 10. Racial variations in the gall bladder. Anat. Rec. 110: 573–90.

Smith, H. W. 1965. The development of the flora of the alimentary tract in young animals. J. Pathol. Bacteriol. 90: 495–513.

Southern, H. N. 1940. Coprophagy in the wild rabbit. Nature (London) 145: 262.

Spector, W. S. 1956. *Handbook of Biological Data*. W. B. Saunders Co.: Philadelphia, Pennsylvania.

Swenson, M. J., ed. 1970. *Duke's Physiology of Domestic Animals*. Cornell Univ. Press: Ithaca, New York.

Thacker, E. J., and C. S. Brandt. 1955. Coprophagy in the rabbit. J. Nutr. 55: 375–85.

Wallace, L. J., and L. R. Arrington. 1968. Absence or anomaly of the gall bladder in domestic rabbits. The Southwestern Vet. 21: 199–200.

Watson, J. S., and R. H. Taylor. 1955. Reingestion in the hare (*Lepus europaeus* Pal.). Science 121: 314.

Weisbroth, S. H., R. E. Flatt, and A. L. Kraus, eds. 1974. *The Biology of the Laboratory Rabbit*. Academic Press: New York.

Wells, T. A. G. 1964. *The Rabbit: A Dissection Manual*. Dover Publications: New York.

Widdowson, E. M. 1950. Chemical composition of newly born mammals. Nature (London) 166: 626–28.

Yoshida, T., J. R. Pleasants, B. S. Reddy, and B. S. Westmann. 1968. Efficiency of digestion in germ-free and conventional rabbits. Brit. J. Nutr. 22: 727–37.

4. REPRODUCTION AND BREEDING

Reproductive processes in the rabbit are basically similar to those in other mammals, but there are some differences peculiar to the species. An understanding of these processes and the special characteristics is important in the management and breeding of rabbits to allow for maximum reproductive rate.

REPRODUCTION IN THE MALE

Major male reproductive organs are the paired testis, the connecting tubules, the accessory sex glands, and the penis (Fig. 4.1). The epididymis, which is a long, convoluted tubule, connects each of the testes with the vas deferens (ductus deferens). The vas deferens leads to the urethra and near their junction are the accessory glands—seminal vesicles (vesicular glands), prostate gland, and bulbo-urethral glands. The urinary bladder joins the urethra, and the urethra serves as a common duct for the delivery of semen and the voiding of urine.

Spermatozoa or male germ cells are formed in each testis. The germ cells are immature upon release from the testes and complete their development in the epididymis. Passage through this structure requires from 4 to 7 days in a rabbit. Secretions from the accessory glands provide a nutrient medium for maintenance and viability of the sperm, and the major portion of semen is made up of these secretions. The volume of semen per ejaculate is about 0.5–1.5 ml. Number of sperm produced per day or per ejaculate varies over a wide range, depending on several factors. The sexually mature New Zealand White male produces about 200 million sperm per day.

REPRODUCTION IN THE FEMALE

Two of the major differences in the reproduction of rabbits from most other mammals are that the female does not exhibit a true estrous cycle and that ovulation is induced rather than spontaneous. Absence of the cycle makes it possible to breed rabbits at practically any time, and the characteristic of induced ovulation provides a means of studying certain aspects of reproduction not possible in other animals.

The major organs of reproduction in the female are the paired ovaries, oviducts (Fallopian tubes), uterus, and vagina (Fig. 4.2). Functions of the female reproductive system are to produce the eggs or ova, nourish and protect fetuses, and provide nourishment after birth through lactation.

OVULATION AND FERTILIZATION

Ovulation occurs about 10 hours after the stimulus of mating or some other stimulus which also induces it. A sterile mating or the activity of one doe riding another will usually cause ovulation. The release of eggs is not spontaneous during the estrus stage of the cycle or just after that stage as it is in females of other species which have regular estrous cycles. Since there is no clearly defined cycle, the doe does not exhibit a distinct heat period. Eggs at various stages of development are present in the ovaries and given the appropriate stimulus, mature eggs are released. Luteinizing hormone from the pituitary gland is released upon the stimulation of mating and acts on the ovarian follicles, bringing about maturation and release of the eggs. At the sites on each ovary where the follicles have ruptured, a structure known as the corpus luteum forms and functions as an endocrine gland, producing the hormone progesterone which is necessary for the maintenance of pregnancy. If there is a sterile mating or if the female is otherwise stimulated to ovulate, she may undergo a stage of pseudopregnancy.

Rabbit eggs are reputed to be the largest so far recorded for mammals and measure about 160 microns in diameter. They are also the fastest developing and are the easiest of mammalian eggs to cultivate through cleavage stages (Adams, 1970a, b). Eggs released from the ovaries are swept into the funnel-like structures (fimbriae) of the oviduct, which is adjacent to and partially sur-

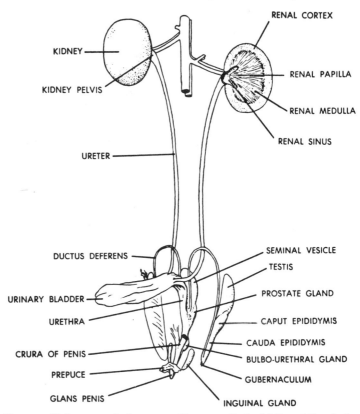

Fig. 4.1. Male urogenital organs. (Source: C. A. McLaughlin, *Laboratory Anatomy of the Rabbit.* Photo copyright © 1970 by the Wm. C. Brown Co., Dubuque, Iowa.)

rounds each ovary. They migrate into the upper portion of the oviduct where fertilization takes place. The eggs remain fertilizable for 6–8 hours after ovulation. Sperm are deposited by the male in the vagina near the cervix, and reach the oviduct 15–30 minutes after mating. The rabbit, along with the chinchilla, has two cervices rather than one as is common in many mammals.

The zygote (fertilized ovum), after reaching the uterus, may not therefore migrate from one horn of the uterus to another as may occur in some other species which have a single cervix. While in the female tract, rabbit sperm must undergo capacitation (changes

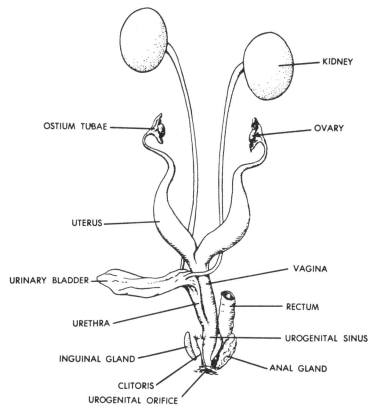

Fig. 4.2. Female urogenital organs. (Source: C. A. McLaughlin, *Laboratory Anatomy of the Rabbit*. Photo copyright © 1970 by the Wm. C. Brown Co., Dubuque, Iowa.)

necessary for capacity to fertilize the eggs). These changes must occur in the female tract and require about 6 hours, but the specific conditions necessary are not clearly established. After fertilization, cell division begins and progresses to about the 8- or 16-cell stage of development (blastocyst) in the oviduct.

IMPLANTATION, GESTATION, AND PARTURITION

The blastocysts reach the uterus on the third or fourth day after mating and for a short time are nourished by fluids (uterine milk) there. Implantation or attachment to the uterine wall takes place during the latter part of the sixth or the early part of the seventh day. Upon implantation, the blastocysts are evenly spaced within each horn of the uterus. The placenta then forms and serves as the life support system for the developing embryo. The placenta, referred to as the afterbirth when it has been expelled following delivery, is the complex structure which connects the developing fetus to the mother and through which nourishment and interchange of all physiological processes for development are accomplished.

Gestation period of the domestic rabbit is usually 31–32 days but may vary between 29 and 35 days. Small litters tend to be carried longer than large litters and individuals in small litters weigh more at birth. Most of the fetal weight at birth is accumulated during the last 14 days of pregnancy. Individual fetal weight is about 1/2–1 gram at midpregnancy, or 16 days, and less than 5 grams at 20 days. At birth the New Zealand rabbit weighs approximately 64 grams.

Parturition or delivery of the young normally takes place in the early morning. Usually it is complete in less than 30 minutes, but occasionally delivery is split by several hours, and there have been cases of young born a day or more apart. At parturition the doe stands in a crouched position with the head between the legs. The mouth is used to assist delivery and to clean the young of the fetal membranes. Although the rabbit is a plant-eating animal, the female usually consumes the placenta and, in so doing, cuts the umbilical cord.

PUBERTY AND BREEDING AGE

Rabbits reach sexual maturity at different ages, depending upon breed, plane of nutrition, and other factors. Small breeds mature earlier than larger ones and females mature earlier than males (Table 4.1). Inadequate nutrition may delay sexual maturity in any breed. Motile sperm may be present in the ejaculate of the males by 4 months of age, but maximum daily sperm production is not normally reached until about 6 months of age.

Although rabbits are capable of reproducing when they reach puberty, it is generally desirable to delay breeding for several weeks. The doe may not have reached mature body size, and

TABLE 4.1. REPRODUCTIVE DATA

Age at puberty, mo.	
New Zealand	
Female	4–5
Male	5–6
Dutch	
Female	3–4
Male	4–5
Breeding age, mo.	
New Zealand	
Female	5.5–6.5
Male	5.5–6.5
Dutch	
Female	4.5–5.5
Male	4.5–5.5
Type of ovulation	induced
Time of ovulation	10 hrs after mating
Fertilization time	1–2 hrs after ovulation
Fertilizable life of ovum	6 hrs
Ovum transit, tube to uterus	3 days
Implantation	7 days after fertilization
Sperm capacitation	6 hrs
Volume of ejaculate	0.5–1.5 ml
Sperm concentration	200 million per ml
Fertilizable life of sperm	30 hrs
Gestation period	31–32 days
Re-bred after kindling	immediate, or at any time if not lactating; 28–42 days if lactating
Birth weight	
New Zealand	64 g
Dutch	40 g
Reproductive life, male and female	1–3 years
Litter size	
Polish, Netherland Dwarf	4 or less
Bevern, Havana, Angora	4–6
Dutch	6–7
Chinchilla, Belgian Hare	6–8
New Zealand, Californian	8–10

often the young doe with her first litter will not prepare a suitable nest or care properly for her offspring. A desirable mating age is 4–5 months for small breeds, 5–7 months for medium breeds, and 8–10 months for large breeds.

LITTER SIZE

The number of young per litter depends upon breed, age of the female, and other factors. Average litter size for several common breeds is indicated in Table 4.1. Number of young per litter tend to increase to the third litter, remain fairly constant for about two years, then decline. Size of litters also appears to be related to the time of year or temperature since the number born per litter tends to be slightly higher during the winter or colder months and lower during the late summer. The normal ratio of males to females is about 53 per cent and 47 per cent, respectively.

MATING RABBITS

The female rabbit does not exhibit a distinct heat period and will mate and conceive at almost any time there is exposure to an aggressive male. Since ovulation occurs about 10 hours after mating, the ova are present in the oviducts at the appropriate time for fertilization. The ability to mate rabbits without having to determine a heat period is a distinct advantage because females may be bred at a time desirable to the producer.

Although females do not exhibit a definite heat period, they often do exhibit a period of activity which indicates a time of receptivity. This is evident by the doe rubbing her chin on the feed cups or other objects and a slight aggressive restlessness. The vulva or external genitalia may be slightly swollen and pink. Breeding at this time will likely be easier and less time-consuming, but it does not indicate the only time that the female will mate. In caged rabbits, the natural courtship or pre-mating behavior is not readily observed. If housed together, or in the wild, courtship chasing occurs, and the males exhibit a characteristic tail flagging. Males may also eject a stream of urine when the caretaker begins the approach of presenting the doe to a buck. Urine discharged at this time may be sprayed some distance into other cages or onto the floor.

When breeding, the female is always taken to the male's cage. The female is aggressive in her own cage or surroundings, and if the buck is placed in her cage, she will in most cases refuse to mate. Copulation normally will take place in a very short time. The buck almost immediately begins rapid copulatory movements, and the female will usually raise her hindquarters to a desirable height for mating. Copulation usually requires only a few seconds and a successful mating is completed when the male falls to one side or backward. At the time of ejaculation, the buck's rear feet are lifted off the floor and he loses his balance. A characteristic cry is often heard and is assumed to be an indication of pain. When mating is complete the female should be returned to her cage.

At times the female will appear to refuse the male. She may move about the cage and cause the male to become partially exhausted from attempting to mate. Even when this occurs, the female may still mate if she is restrained. In some cases it may be necessary to hold the doe and raise the hindquarters to the normal height for service (Fig. 4.3). In either case, a successful mating is indicated by the male falling to one side. Occasionally a female will not mate even though restrained. In such a case it is better to return her to her cage and make another attempt on the next day.

Some breeders have made it a practice to breed the female a second time several hours after the first under the assumption that better conception rates will result from two matings. Studies have indicated, however, that there is no advantage in a second mating as the sperm cells from the first mating remain viable for a number of hours.

The dates of all matings should be recorded so that scheduled littering times are known. It is a good practice to mate several does on the same day or near the same time so that fostering of the young can be accomplished more readily if it is necessary.

DIAGNOSING PREGNANCY

Once the female is mated it is desirable to know whether she has conceived, for all matings do not produce pregnancies. If a female is assumed pregnant but is not and no test is made, then it will not be known until the time for the delivery has passed. This can result in a considerable loss of time; therefore, testing which will detect pregnancy in the early stages is desirable. Abdominal palpation is the common method, but it is not reliable until about midpregnancy. A biological laboratory test can detect pregnancy

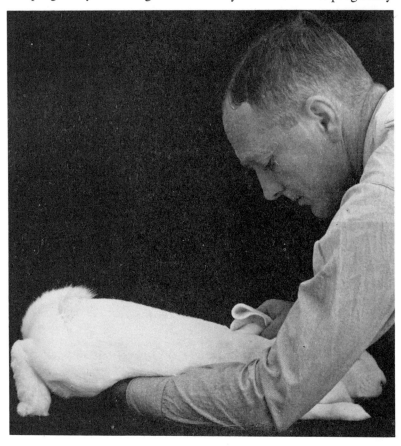

Fig. 4.3. Restraint of female for mating. (Photo courtesy U.S. Department of Agriculture.)

in the early stages, but this requires specific training, is expensive, and would not be practical in most cases except perhaps for those rabbits that are used in research.

Palpation involves careful feeling of the abdomen for evidence of the embryos. Before attempting the procedure, the beginner should learn what he is expected to feel and where the embryos are located. The rabbit uterus has two divisions (horns), one on each side of the abdomen. Embryos will be in both horns in most pregnancies and are evenly spaced in the tubular uterine bodies. At about 15–16 days, each embryo and the supporting structure is about the size of a marble, and they may be felt and distinguished from the other internal structures.

The female is placed on a table or surface where she can be easily handled. With the rabbit held in a normal and relaxed position the hand is placed under and around the abdomen (Fig. 4.4). The thumb and forefinger or middle finger should be used to feel the embryos by moving the hand gently backward and forward. If the female is pregnant and the pregnancy has progressed to about midterm or later, the embryos should be easily felt as distinct "balls" or structures evenly spaced on each side. Detection is easier in the later stages of pregnancy. Considerable experience is required for any degree of accuracy in pregnancy detection, and the beginner should not expect to be proficient with the first few attempts.

GESTATION AND KINDLING

During pregnancy no special handling is generally required for the doe other than routine good care and feeding. Does should be observed regularly for any evidence of abnormality. No special feed is necessary if normal feed is of good quality and supplies a balanced diet. During the last two weeks of gestation and during lactation, does will need a full feed of good quality. If the previous diet was largely hay or low in protein, then it should be changed to one including at least 15 per cent protein.

Two or three days prior to scheduled littering, the nest box (chapter 8) should be provided. It should be partly filled with

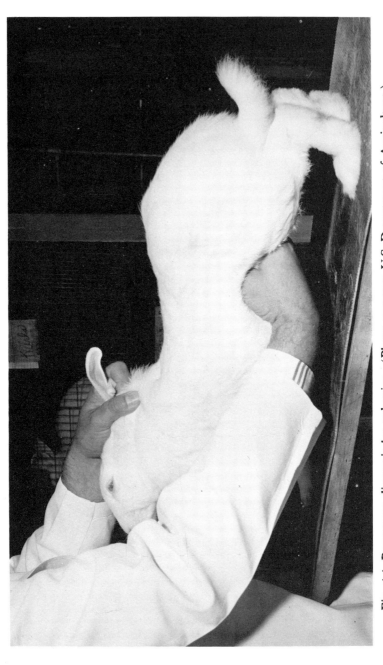

Fig. 4.4. Pregnancy diagnosis by palpation. (Photo courtesy U.S. Department of Agriculture.)

hay, straw, or some other bedding material. If a nest box is not provided and the female delivers her young on the floor of the hutch, they will frequently be trampled and likely abandoned. Before kindling, the female will move about the cage with a mouth full of hay, preparing a nest. Shortly before parturition she may pull hair from her chest and abdomen to line the nest. The mammary system develops rapidly during the last week of gestation and occasionally milk will leak from the glands in high-producing females. Females having their first litter occasionally fail to prepare a proper nest. The quality of nests improves, however, with later litters.

At the time of parturition it is best to leave the female alone except for routine care and feeding. On the day after birth of the litter, the nest should be examined and any dead or abnormal young removed. The nest should be checked daily or every other day for several days with as little disturbance to the female as possible.

Occasionally, a female will have her young outside of the nest box even though it was provided in ample time. This occurs more often with the first litter females than with the older ones. Most of these litters will survive if found early after birth and placed in the box.

Rabbits are born hairless, blind, and helpless. They develop rapidly with adequate care and lactation of the female and double their weight in about a week. Eyes open about the tenth day and the young begin leaving the nest and eating dry feed at about 3 weeks.

LACTATION

Lactation is initiated at parturition and continues for 6–8 weeks provided the doe is nursing young. The amount of milk produced increases for about 2 weeks, remains high for another 2 weeks, and begins to decline at about 4 weeks. Average daily milk yield for does of medium-weight breeds is 170–220 grams per day, but is slightly less with the first litter. Females vary widely in the amount of milk produced, and this has a definite effect upon the weight of young at weaning. The selection of breeding females which are good milk producers is important. Since the weight of young rabbits at 3 weeks of age is due in large part to milk consumed, the comparative weight of litters at this time (assuming equal litter size) is a good measure of milk production.

Rabbits nurse their young only once daily, usually at night or in the early morning. They are seldom seen in the nest box as nursing requires only a few minutes; this often leads to concern by beginning producers that the doe is not caring for her young. Evidence of proper feeding can be seen by examining the young and doe. Stomachs of the young should show signs of containing milk, and the mammary glands of the female should be filled but not hard. The normal number of mammary glands is eight. If it appears that the female is not nursing the litter, she should be examined for mammary abnormalities (chapter 7). Under certain conditions, young may be fostered on another lactating female if necessary. Artificial feeding is possible but generally not practical with rabbits. If a doe fails to feed her litter, attempts to force her to do so are usually not successful.

The composition of rabbit milk and its comparison with that of other species is indicated in Table 4.2. Percentage composition of the nutrients varies widely at different stages of lactation. Of particular interest is the decrease in fat toward the middle of lactation, followed by an increase near the termination. The total dry matter content of about 35 per cent shows rabbit milk to be one of the most concentrated of those species studied. Near the termination of lactation, dry matter may approach 50 per cent.

FOSTERING YOUNG

Fostering simply means the transfer of one or more nursing young from one female to another lactating female. This may be necessary if a nursing doe dies, fails to lactate normally, or has produced more offspring than she can feed properly. In some cases, a doe may have only a small litter of her own, and it is desirable to give her more young so that the milk produced can be adequately removed, thus aiding in the prevention of caked udders. A desirable number of young for females of medium-weight breeds to nurse is eight. Does may successfully feed more than eight, but if there are many more, the size of individual young at weaning time may be smaller than normal. When fostering is practiced the transfer should be made when the rabbits are as young as possible, and they should be given to a doe that has a litter of about the same age as those being transferred. Litters born as much as 3 days apart may be successfully placed together. Fostering generally may be carried out when the young are up to about 2 weeks old. If they are older, it is less likely that

TABLE 4.2. COMPOSITION OF MILK, PER CENT

Animal	Water	Protein	Lactose	Fat	Ash
Rabbit					
Colostrum	68	13.5	1.6	14.7	1.6
14 days	74	13.4	1.0	9.0	2.2
30 days	63	16.9	0.2	17.5	2.8
Cow	87	3.5	4.8	4.0	0.7
Human	87	1.2	6.9	4.6	0.2
Sheep	84	4.8	4.6	5.4	0.9
Goat	87	3.7	4.2	4.1	0.8
Pig	84	4.9	5.3	5.3	0.9

SOURCES: Rabbit data adapted from Lebas, 1971; other data represent averages from Dittmer, 1961.

the foster mother will accept them. Fortunately, most foster does will accept young from another and usually there are no problems. If it is necessary to keep records of the parentage of those transferred, the young should be identified in some way. When making the transfer, the doe should be disturbed as little as possible.

Caution should be exercised in fostering young from a mother which has died from an unknown cause. These should be transferred to one other doe only. If the death resulted from an infectious disease, the young could be infected, and by transferring them to only one doe, the possible spread could be limited to one female. Young from the female which received the orphans could be redistributed to other does.

CARE OF LITTERS

If a satisfactory nest box has been provided, and the doe is fed properly and is lactating and feeding her young, there is little else that needs to be done for the litter. The nest box should be inspected regularly to check the condition of the young. As always, this inspection should be done carefully and with little disturbance to the female. Occasionally, the female will begin to urinate and defecate in the nest box. Once she has started this habit, it is very difficult to stop the practice. It can become a problem since it is preferable not to disturb the young by moving them to another box. Usually the feces and urine are deposited away from the nest and the young may remain there for several days. At that time it may be necessary to transfer them to a clean box with fresh bedding and some of the clean hair from the previous nest. Occasionally, the doe will stop depositing excreta in the new nest box; if she continues, the box should be cleaned periodically.

Young rabbits grow rapidly when they get adequate milk. At about 3 weeks they become quite active and begin to come out of the nest box. At this time also, they begin to nibble some of the mother's feed. Some producers make a practice of creep feeding the young before weaning (chapter 6).

When the litter is about 5 weeks old, the nest box should be removed. In cold weather it may remain longer for protection, but in hot weather the box should be removed to provide more floor space and better ventilation in the cage. In very hot weather, a wire nest box may be desirable to increase cooling by permitting better ventilation.

WEANING

The traditional practice for medium-weight breeds has been to wean or remove the young from a doe at about 8 weeks of age. Experiments have shown, however, that young may be weaned successfully at 4 weeks of age with creep feeding. Without creep feed, New Zealand and Dutch have been successfully weaned at

4 weeks, but by 8 weeks they were not as heavy as those that had remained with the doe for that period. When young are removed earlier than 8 weeks, the female may be re-bred earlier and this is an advantage. In practice, weaning at 6–7 weeks is quite satisfactory. With the early weaning it is desirable to remove the larger, faster-growing young first and leave the small ones. This provides more milk for those growing more slowly and prevents the swollen or caked udders which could result from abrupt early weaning. Rabbits weaned at 6–8 weeks should be able to consume the regular feeds supplied to adults, and no creep feed should be necessary.

SEXING RABBITS

Identification of the sex of most animals is relatively easy, but in the young or prepubertal animal and even in the adults of those covered with hair, a close examination is necessary to distinguish the sexes. In the adult male the inguinal pouches, which are hairless, are located on each side of the genital area and are easily seen. In the rabbit's normal standing or sitting position, however, these may not be visible, and the animal must be held for examination. Prior to about 4–6 weeks, the testicles are retained in the body cavity and the inguinal pouches are harder to see. In order to sex a young rabbit, it is necessary to make a very close examination. The fingers are placed before and behind the genital area and with a little pressure the inner surface of the genital organ is exposed. In the female the opening is slit-like and slopes toward the anus (Fig. 4.5). The male organ protrudes slightly and appears rounded. Rabbits as young as 2–3 days may be sexed in this way. In learning the procedure it is best to begin with older animals and compare the sexes so that differences are readily seen.

ARTIFICIAL INSEMINATION

Artificial insemination of cattle and some other species of animals is practiced widely and has a distinct advantage in extending the genetic influence of desirable males. Rabbits may be bred arti-

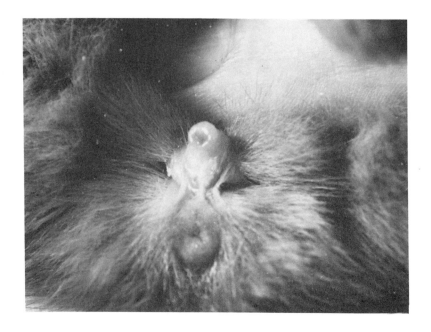

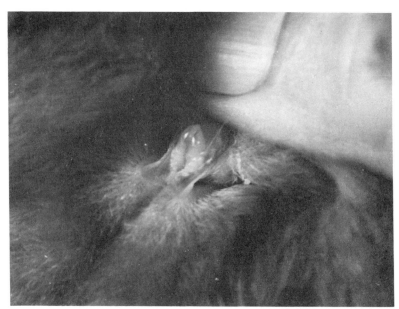

Fig. 4.5. Sex differences in external genitalia of young rabbits. Upper, male. Lower, female. (Photos copyright © 1972 by the Interstate Printers and Publishers, Danville, Ill.)

ficially, but it is not a general practice except in special situations and in experimental work. The time required to collect the semen, process it, and inseminate the female, combined with the technical training necessary, makes the procedure generally impractical.

Semen is collected in an artificial vagina, which is usually held under a frame covered with a rabbit skin simulating another rabbit. Mature males which have mated previously can be trained to mount the skin and ejaculate into the artificial vagina. The semen may be used directly for insemination of one or more females, it may be diluted for use with a larger number of does, or, with appropriate treatment, it may be frozen and stored for later use. The doe must be stimulated to ovulate and this is usually done at the time of insemination. Mating with a vasectomized male or injecting luteinizing hormone may induce ovulation. The semen is deposited in the vagina near the cervix by means of a plastic or glass tube. In experimental work, insemination may be made into the uterus surgically or by intraperitoneal injection into the abdominal cavity. Techniques of the procedures for semen collection and insemination as well as procedures for embryo transfer are described by Hafez (1970).

PSEUDOPREGNANCY

Pseudopregnancy or false pregnancy refers to a condition resembling that of early pregnancy. It can occur in rabbits and several other species of animals. In rabbits it may result from a sterile mating or stimulation caused when one doe has mounted another or even when the doe mounts the young in her own litter. This stimulation induces ovulation and formation of the corpus luteum which produces the hormone progesterone, causing the reproductive tract to act for a time as though the female is pregnant. Pseudopregnancy lasts 16–17 days, during which time the doe will not mate. The mammary glands enlarge to some extent and the female may pull hair and begin preparation for the nest. The condition frequently occurs in mature female rabbits housed together. Those that are to be bred should be removed from groups to individual cages for at least 16 days before they are mated. Pseudopregnancy is not harmful to the doe and it does not indicate that she is abnormal; it is a disadvantage in terms of breeding since conception cannot occur during this period, and the time of breeding is delayed.

REFERENCES

Adams, C. E. 1960. Prenatal mortality in the rabbit. J. Reprod. Fert. 1: 36–44.

Adams, C. E. 1960. Studies on prenatal mortality in the rabbit (*O. Cuniculus*): The amount and distribution of loss before and after implantation. J. Endocr. 19: 325–44.

Adams, C. E. 1961. Artificial insemination in the rabbit. J. Reprod. Fert. 2: 521–22.

Adams, C. E. 1967. Concurrent lactation and pregnancy in the rabbit. J. Reprod. Fert. 14: 351–52.

Adams, C. E. 1969. Intraperitoneal insemination in the rabbit. J. Reprod. Fert. 18: 333–39.

Adams, C. E. 1970a. Ageing and reproduction in the female mammal with particular reference to the rabbit. J. Reprod. Fert. Suppl. 12: 1–16.

Adams, C. E. 1970b. The development of rabbit eggs after culture *in vitro* for 1–4 days. J. Embryol. Exp. Morph. 23: 21–34.

Adams, C. E., and M. C. Chang. 1962. Capacitation of rabbit spermatozoa in the fallopian tube and in the uterus. J. Exp. Zool. 143: 26–28.

Amann, R. P. 1966. Effect of ejaculation frequency and breed on semen characteristics and sperm output of rabbits. J. Reprod. Fert. 11: 291–93.

Amann, R. P. 1970. The male rabbit. 4. Quantitative testicular histology and comparisons between daily sperm production as determined histologically and daily sperm output. Fertil. Steril. 21: 662–72.

Amann, R. P., and J. T. Lambiase. 1969. The male rabbit. 3. Determination of daily sperm production by means of testicular homogenates. J. Anim. Sci. 28: 369–74.

Bedford, J. M. 1971. The rate of sperm passage into the cervix after coitus in the rabbit. J. Reprod. Fert. 25: 211–18.

Beyer, C., and N. Rivaud. 1969. Sexual behavior in pregnant and lactating domestic rabbits. Physiol. Behav. 4: 753–57.

Brackett, B. G., and J. B. Server. 1970. Capacitation of rabbit spermatozoa in the uterus. Fertil. Steril. 21: 687–95.

Breed, W. G., and J. Hillard. 1970. Effect of lactation on ovarian function in the rabbit. J. Reprod. Fert. 23: 73–78.

Breederman, P. J., R. H. Foote, and A. M. Yassen. 1964. An improved artificial vagina for collecting rabbit semen. J. Reprod. Fert. 7: 401–3.

Chang, M. C., and A. L. Southern. 1970. The fertilizing life of spermatozoa in the female tract of rabbits and ferrets treated with oestrogen. J. Reprod. Fert. 23: 173–75.

Coates, M. E., M. E. Gregory, and S. Y. Thompson. 1964. The composition of rabbit's milk. Brit. J. Nutr. 18: 583–86.

Cowie, A. T. 1969. Variations in the yield and composition of the milk during lactation in the rabbit and the galactopoietic effect of prolactin. J. Endocrin. 44: 437–50.

Cross, B. A. 1958. On the mechanism of labor in the rabbit. J. Endocrin. 16: 261.

Denenberg, V. H., P. B. Sawin, B. P. Frommer, and S. Ross. 1958. Genetic, physiological and behavioral background of reproduction in the rabbit. 4. Analysis of maternal behavior at successive parturitions. Behavior 13: 131–42.

Desjardins, C., K. T. Kirton, and H. D. Hafs. 1968. Sperm output of rabbits at various ejaculation frequencies and their use in the design of experiments. J. Reprod. Fert. 15: 27–32.

DiLella, T., and L. Zicarelli. 1971. Milk production of New Zealand White rabbits. (Text in Italian, English summary.) Riv. Zootec. 44: 85–97.

Doggett, V. C. 1956. Periodicity in the fecundity of male rabbits. Am. J. Physiol. 187: 445–50.

El-Banna, A. A., and E. S. E. Hafez. 1970. Sperm transport and distribution in rabbit and cattle female tracts. Fertil. Steril. 21: 534–40.

Fox, R. R. 1961. Preservation of rabbit spermatozoa: Fertility results from frozen semen. Proc. Soc. Exp. Biol. Med. 108: 663–65.

Fox, R. R., and J. F. Burdick. 1963. Preservation of rabbit spermatozoa: Ethylene glycol vs. glycerol for frozen semen. Proc. Soc. Exp. Biol. Med. 113: 853–56.

Fox, R. R., and D. D. Crary. 1972. A simple technique for the sexing of newborn rabbits. Lab. Anim. Sci. 22: 556–58.

Foxcroft, G. R., and T. O'Shea. 1973. Effects of suckling and time to mating after parturition on reproduction in the domestic rabbit. J. Reprod. Fert. 33: 367–77.

Fussel, E. N., J. D. Roussel, and C. R. Austin. 1966. Single-handed artificial insemination of rabbits. J. Inst. Anim. Tech. 17: 103–5.

Gregorie, A. T., R. W. Bratton, and R. H. Foote. 1958. Sperm output and fertility of rabbits ejaculated either once a week or once a day for forty-three weeks. J. Anim. Sci. 17: 243–48.

Gregory, P. W. 1932. The potential and actual fecundity of some breeds of rabbits. J. Exp. Zool. 62: 271–85.

Gulyos, B. J. 1968. Effects of ageing on fertilizing capacity and morphology of rabbit sperm. Fertil. Steril. 19: 453–61.

Hafez, E. S. E., ed. 1970. *Reproduction and Breeding Techniques for Laboratory Animals.* Lea and Febiger: Philadelphia, Pennsylvania.

Hafez, E. S. E., D. D. Lindsay, and L. A. Moustafa. 1967. Effects of feed intake of pregnant rabbits on nutrition reserves of neonates. Am. J. Vet. Res. 28: 1153–59.

Hammer, C. E., and N. J. Sojka. 1968. Requirements for capacitation of rabbit sperm. Nature (London) 220: 1042–43.

Harned, M. A., and L. E. Casida. 1969. Some postpartum reproductive phenomena in the domestic rabbit. J. Anim. Sci. 28: 785–88.

Hays, R. L., and K. A. Kendall. 1956. The beneficial effect of progesterone on pregnancy in the vitamin A deficient rabbit. J. Nutr. 59: 337–42.

Holtz, W., and R. H. Foote. 1972. Sperm production, output and urinary loss in the rabbit. Proc. Soc. Exp. Biol. Med. 141: 958–62.

Kaufman, A. F., K. D. Quist, and J. R. Broderson. 1971. Pseudopregnancy in the New Zealand White rabbit: Necropsy findings. Lab. Anim. Sci. 21: 865–69.

Kendall, K. A., R. L. Hays, and G. D. Rolleri. 1954. Impaired reproduction in the rabbit fed supplemented diets containing soybean hay. J. Anim. Sci. 13: 859–66.

Koefoed-Johnsen, H. H., A. Pavlok, and J. Fulka. 1971. The influence of ageing of rabbit spermatozoa *in vitro* on fertilizing capacity and embryonic mortality. J. Reprod. Fert. 26: 351–56.

Larson, L. L., C. H. Spilman, and H. O. Dunn. 1973. Reproductive efficiency in aged female rabbits given supplemental progesterone and oestradiol. J. Reprod. Fert. 33: 31–38.

Lebas, F. 1970. Feeding and growth of suckling rabbits. (Text in French.) Rec. Med. Vet. 146: 1065–70.

Lebas, F. 1970. A milking machine for rabbits. (Text in French, English summary.) Ann. Zootech. 19: 223–28.

Lebas, F. 1971. Composition chimique du lait de lapine, evolution au cours de la traite et el fonction du state de lactation. (English summary.) Ann. Zootech. 21: 185–91.

Lu, M. H., and R. R. Anderson. 1973. Growth of the mammary gland during pregnancy and lactation in the rabbit. Biol. Reprod. 9: 538–43.

MacMillan, K. L., and H. D. Hafs. 1967. Semen output of rabbits ejaculated after varying sexual preparation. Proc. Soc. Exp. Biol. Med. 125: 1278–81.

Matzke, P., and M. Stolzman. 1964. On the effect of artificial insemination of Angora rabbits over a long period: Experience in a 13-year study. (Text in German.) Bayer. Landv. Jb. 41: 387–94.

Menzies, W. 1959. The effect of weaning age on weight gain in rabbits. J. Anim. Tech. Assn. 9: 59–61.

Miller, O. C., J. F. Roche, and D. J. Dziuk. 1969. Estimation of the optimum interval between insemination and ovulation in the rabbit by double insemination. J. Reprod. Fert. 19: 545–46.

Morgan, D. R. 1973. Routine birth induction in rabbits using oxytocin. Lab. Anim. Sci. 8: 127–30.

Morton, D. B., and T. D. Glover. 1974. Sperm transport in the female rabbit: The effect of inseminate volume and sperm density. J. Reprod. Fert. 38: 139–46.

Morton, D. B., and T. D. Glover. 1974. Sperm transport in the female rabbit: The role of the cervix. J. Reprod. Fert. 38: 131–38.

Myers, K., and W. E. Poole. 1962. Oestrus cycles in the rabbit (*Oryctolagus cuniculus* L.). Nature (London) 195: 358–59.

Mykytowycz, R., and P. J. Fullagar. 1973. Effect of social environment on reproduction in the rabbit (*O. cuniculus* L.). J. Reprod. Fert. (Suppl.) 19: 503–22.

Napier, R. A. N. 1961. Fertility in the male rabbit. 1. Sensitivity of spermatozoa to handling techniques. J. Reprod. Fert. 2: 246–59.

Napier, R. A. N. 1961. Fertility in the male rabbit. 2. Variation in the percentage of eggs fertilized. J. Reprod. Fert. 2: 260–72.

Napier, R. A. N. 1961. Fertility in the male rabbit. 3. Estimation of spermatozoan quality by mixed insemination and the inheritance of spermatozoan characters. J. Reprod. Fert. 2: 273–89.

Noyes, R. W., A. Walton, and C. E. Adams. 1958. Capacitation of rabbit spermatozoa. Nature (London) 181: 1209–10.

Overstreet, J. W. 1970. Sperm numbers and fertilization in the rabbit. J. Reprod. Fert. 21: 279–88.

Overstreet, J. W., and C. E. Adams. 1971. Mechanisms of selective fertilization in the rabbit: Sperm transport and viability. J. Reprod. Fert. 26: 219–31.

Plotka, E. D., and W. L. Williams. 1971. Hormones and sperm capacitation in rabbits. Proc. Soc. Exp. Biol. Med. 136: 934–36.

Rathore, A. K. 1970. High temperature exposure of male rabbits. Indian Vet. J. 47: 837–40.

Rich, T. D., and C. W. Alliston. 1970. Influence of programmed circadian temperature changes on the reproductive performance of rabbits acclimated to two different temperatures. J. Anim. Sci. 30: 960–65.

Ross, S., P. B. Sawin, M. X. Zarrow, and V. H. Denenberg. 1963. Maternal behavior in the rabbit. In *Maternal Behavior in Mammals*, ed. H. L. Rheingold. John Wiley and Sons: New York.

Sittman, D. B., W. C. Rollins, K. Sittman, and R. B. Casady. 1964. Seasonal variation in reproductive traits of New Zealand White rabbits. J. Reprod. Fert. 8: 29–37.

Soupart, P. 1970. Leukocytes and sperm capacitation in the rabbit uterus. Fertil. Steril. 21: 724–56.

Stranzinger, G. F., R. R. Maurer, and S. K. Paufler. 1971. Fertility of frozen rabbit semen. J. Reprod. Fert. 24: 111–13.

Suitor, A. E. 1946. Palpating domestic rabbits to determine pregnancy. Leaflet 245. U.S. Department of Agriculture: Washington, D.C.

Tesh, J. M. 1969. Effects of ageing of rabbit spermatozoa *in utero* on fertilization and prenatal development. J. Reprod. Fert. 20: 299–306.

Tesh, J. M., and T. D. Glover. 1969. Ageing of rabbit spermatozoa in the male tract and its effect on fertility. J. Reprod. Fert. 20: 287–97.

Vander Vliet, W. L., and E. S. E. Hafez. 1974. The fertilizing life of spermatozoa in the rabbit oviduct. J. Anim. Sci. 39: 373–79.

Venge, O. 1963. The influence of nursing behavior and milk production on early growth in rabbits. Anim. Behavior 11: 500–506.

Wales, R. G., and T. O'Shea. 1968. The deep freezing of rabbit spermatozoa. Aust. J. Biol. Sci. 21: 831–33.

Walter, M. R., L. Martiner, B. Moret, and C. Thibault. 1968. Photoperiodic regulation of sexual activity in the male and female rabbit. Arch. Anat. Histol. Embryol. 51: 773–80.

Zarrow, M. X., V. H. Denenberg, and C. O. Anderson. 1965. Rabbit: Frequency of suckling in the pup. Science 150: 1835–36.

5. GENETICS AND ANIMAL IMPROVEMENT

Genetics is the science which deals with the transmission of hereditary characteristics from one generation to the next. The laws of inheritance apply to rabbits in the same way that they apply to other animals. A knowledge of these laws is important in understanding variations in body type, coat color, growth and body size, number of young per litter, and abnormalities. Variations found in some characteristics can also result from environmental influences, such as the effect of level of nutrition on growth as well as reproduction. The differences observed in certain traits, therefore, may be due to genetic as well as environmental influences which allow expression of the character. A survey of the principles of genetics and of breeding systems useful in improving rabbit characteristics will be presented in this chapter.

BASIC PRINCIPLES OF INHERITANCE

Rabbits, like other mammals, are made up of a large number of individual cells varying in size, type, and function. An important aspect of these cells is that each contains genetic material which is similar to that in every other cell in the same animal. This genetic material is composed of many small units referred to as *genes*. They are located in the nucleus of the cell and are carried on long, thread-like bodies called *chromosomes*, which occur in pairs and whose number varies from one species to another. In the rabbit there are 44 chromosomes, or 22 pairs. Chromosomes in the nucleus of cells may be observed by use of special laboratory techniques. A display (karyotype) of rabbit chromosomes illustrating relative size and structure is shown in Figure 5.1.

Genes also occur in pairs, and genes on the chromosomes are transmitted from parent to offspring in sex cells known as

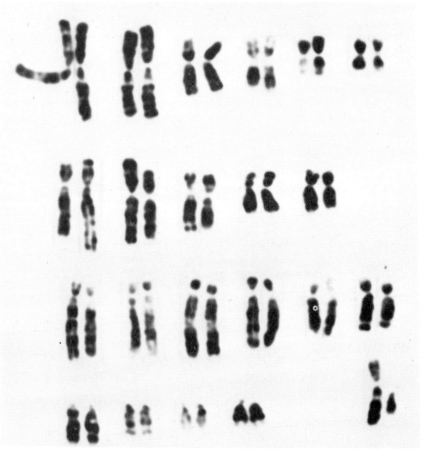

Fig. 5.1. Karyotype of the rabbit. G-bands, male. (Photo courtesy A. Dean Stock, Anderson Hospital, University of Texas, Houston.)

gametes. Male gametes are known as *spermatozoa* and female gametes as *ova* or eggs. Spermatozoa are formed in the seminiferous tubules of the testes by the process of *spermatogenesis.* Ova formation in the germinal layer of the ovary is known as *oogenesis.* One of the steps involved in the formation of gametes is separation of the paired chromosomes and formation of new cells having only one member of each pair. This process of forming new gametes having only a random one-half of the chromosomes is called *meiosis*. At fertilization, male and female gametes unite and the regular number of chromosomes is restored. In this manner, the number of chromosomes in the offspring remains constant from generation to generation. Most basic genetics books explain these processes in more detail (Herskowitz, 1965).

One pair of chromosomes (commonly referred to as the X and Y) are involved in sex determination of an individual. If two X chromosomes are paired at fertilization the individual will be a female; if an X and Y chromosome are paired, the individual will be a male. The female can transmit only X chromosomes to her progeny, but the male can transmit either the X or Y. Normally, XX and XY pairs occur and thus the gamete from the male determines the sex of the offspring.

There are large numbers of genes on each chromosome in the rabbit. Genes on the same chromosome are called linked genes and tend to be inherited together, because they go to the same gamete as a unit (genes and chromosome). The first evidence of gene linkage in the rabbit was reported by Castle (1924). Robinson (1956) presented a summary of known linkage groups in rabbits. The only way for two linked genes to become separated is for a crossover to occur during cell division when two paired chromosomes exchange parts of their chromosomes and thus exchange genes.

Genes that are on the sex chromosomes (X and Y) are referred to as sex-linked. Genes on X chromosomes in the female function as those on the other twenty-one pairs of chromosomes. However, the genes on the X chromosome in males function as a single gene because very few genes are known to exist on the Y chromosome as pairs with those on the X.

CHEMICAL NATURE OF GENES

Prior to 1950, genes were generally thought to be intact units on chromosomes and to be inherited as such. Little was known about the internal structure of genes or chromosomes. Much research has since been carried out, and it is now well known that genes and chromosomes are made up of a chemical substance known as deoxyribonucleic acid (DNA).

The initial work on gene structure was reported by Watson and Crick (1953). Since then extensive research has been reported concerning mechanisms by which DNA controls body function through protein synthesis. In general, the DNA molecule is pictured as two chains wrapped or coiled around each other and hooked together by purine and pyrimidine bases at intervals along the coil or helical structure. The sequence of these bases along one side of the helical DNA molecule serves as the genetic code in directing all physiological functions of the individual cell, the tissue, or the organ to which the cell belongs and ultimately the entire body. Physiological functions occur because of the presence of specific proteins which act as catalysts in various reactions of metabolic pathways. Proteins are synthesized at particular sites in the cell under the direction of ribonucleic acid (RNA), which acts as a messenger in "reading" the genetic code of DNA and processing that message in the form of proteins for subsequent physiological action.

INHERITANCE OF CHARACTERS

Characteristics which show variability in animals are controlled by one or many pairs of genes. Traits such as coat colors or abnormalities, as well as some blood constituents, are controlled by one, two, or three pairs of genes. Growth rate, litter size, mature weight, and lactational ability are traits that are controlled by several and possibly many pairs of genes. The aggregate of genes that controls a particular character is known as the *genotype* of that character. The response or characteristic that is visibly observed in animals—size, color, type, etc.—is called the *phenotype*.

Qualitative Inheritance

Traits such as coat color or fur type that are separated into distinct phenotypic classes and controlled by a few pairs of genes are called qualitative characters. Genes that control qualitative characters have been given letter codes. An example is the two genes controlling color in rabbits: *C* for full body color (the actual color depending upon other genes which control that character) and *c* for albinism (absence of color). Because genes occur in pairs, combinations of the two genes which can occur on paired chromosomes are *CC*, *Cc*, and *cc*. When similar genes are paired (*CC* or *cc*), the pairs are called *homozygous*. When dissimilar genes (*Cc*) are paired, the pair is called *heterozygous*. In rabbits, the heterozygous genotype for body color, *Cc*, appears phenotypically exactly like the homozygous genotype for full body color, *CC*. Thus the *C* gene dominates the *c* gene and controls the phenotypic expression. The *C* gene is said to be *dominant* and the *c* gene *recessive*. Dominant gene symbols for other characteristics are also generally written with capital letters and recessive gene symbols with small letters.

The genetic combination resulting from mating a *CC* male (full body color) to a *cc* female (absence of color) is simple to follow. The male gamete would contain a *C* gene and the female gamete a *c* gene, because only one member of each gene pair is transmitted to the offspring at fertilization. Therefore, the genotype of the progeny from a *CC* x *cc* cross would always be *Cc*, and the phenotype would always be full body color.

If a *Cc* male is mated to a *Cc* female, male and female gametes will be *C* and *c* and will occur with equal frequency. Genotypes and expected body color (phenotype) of progeny from this mating can be seen in the chart.

		Female gametes	
		1/2 *C*	1/2 *c*
Male gametes	1/2 *C*	1/4 *CC* Color	1/4 *Cc* Color
	1/2 *c*	1/4 *Cc* Color	1/4 *cc* White

Note that the frequency of occurrence of the gametes has been added and that this is useful in predicting the frequency of genotypes and phenotypes expected in the progeny. From the chart it can be seen that the genotypes have a predicted frequency occurrence of 1/4 *CC*, 1/2 *Cc*, and 1/4 *cc* or a ratio of 1:2:1. These expectations are possible because it is known that male and female gametes combine randomly. Since the *C* gene was dominant over the recessive *c*, the phenotypic ratio would be expected to be 3/4 color:1/4 albino, or 3:1. The *Cc* genotype would appear exactly as the *CC* genotype, making the two phenotypes indistinguishable. Following similar procedures it is easy to compute expected ratios from other crosses, such as *CC* x *Cc*, *cc* x *Cc*, etc.

The inheritance of two independent qualitative characters can be shown by extending the concept of inheritance for more than one character. Independently inherited characters are those whose controlling genes are located on different pairs of chromosomes. Consider the example of a second pair of genes controlling the color pattern: *A* for agouti (the wild type color pattern) and *a* for self or solid body color such as black. The agouti gene *A* is dominant over *a*. An illustration of the two-character problem would be the mating of homozygous parents, *AACC* male x *aacc* female. Gametes produced by the male would be *AC* because the genes in each pair are identical and only one gene of each pair can be transmitted in the gamete. All female gametes would be *ac*; therefore, all progeny from this cross would be *AaCc* because of the union of *AC* and *ac* gametes at fertilization. The problem becomes slightly more complex when dihybrid matings occur: *AaCc* male x *AaCc* female. Gametes produced by the male and female would be *AC*, *Ac*, *aC*, and *ac*, occurring in equal frequencies. This results because the genes combine randomly in gamete formation when they are located on separate chromosomes. Nine different genotypes can exist in progeny from a dihybrid x dihybrid mating. As a result of the action between the two pairs of genes, three different phenotypes are expected in the progeny, each with a different frequency. The phenotypic array of progeny expected from the above mating would be 9/16 agouti, 3/16 black, and 4/16 albino or a 9:3:4 ratio. It should be pointed out that one of the characters (albino or noncolored) chosen for this example occurs more frequently in rabbits than other mammals. The type of gene action expressed in the example presented is known as *recessive epistasis*. Epistasis is a type of gene action in which one pair of genes exerts influence on another pair of genes. When white, *cc*, is in the homozygous condition, the agouti gene, *A*, or the nonagouti gene, *a*, is not allowed to express its effect due to an epistatic influence of the white genotype.

The inheritance of coat color in rabbits has been of interest to a number of investigators. Reviews on the subject have been presented by Castle (1940) and Searle (1968). Fox (1974), in a discussion of genetics of the rabbit, listed genes and genotypes responsible for the various color patterns of American breeds of rabbits.

Other characteristics which are qualitatively inherited and are of importance to rabbit breeders include those which appear as abnormalities. A detailed review of research findings relating to these abnormalities has been presented by Lindsey and Fox (1974). Most of these disease conditions and anatomical variations are known to exist only in laboratory populations and not in commercial stocks. The rabbit breeder who finds abnormalities appearing in litters can generally decrease the frequency of undesirable genes by culling litters into which abnormal individuals are born as well as culling parents of the litter.

Blood groups in the rabbit also are considered to be qualitative traits since they are controlled by a relatively small number of gene pairs. A review of the major blood groups in rabbits has been reported by Cohen (1962).

Quantitative Inheritance

It was indicated earlier that some characters are influenced by environmental as well as hereditary factors. These traits generally can be classified as having continuous variation because they cannot be assigned to specific groups such as fur color or blood types. Growth rate, milk yield, litter size, age at puberty, and mature size are characters influenced by quantitative inheritance. Genetic variation in these traits is probably due to many pairs of genes with different effects (Falconer, 1960). Those which control most of the variation are known as major genes and those with less influence as minor or modifying genes.

Quantitative characters, those which have continuous variation, tend to follow a normal distribution, that is, the observations when plotted tend to form a bell-shaped curve. Using litter size as an example, a large number of litters from medium-size breeds would be expected to contain 7 or 8 young. A few litters will have only 1 and a few will have 15 or 16. In between the average and the extremes would be a distribution of other litter sizes.

Genetic, phenotypic, and environmental variability are involved in quantitative inheritance. It has already been noted that phenotypic response is a function of genetic plus environmental factors. It can also be established that phenotypic variability is a function of genetic and environmental variability. Genetic variability is usually expressed, for practical purposes, as a ratio to phenotypic variability and is called heritability when expressed as a per cent. Only a few heritability estimates for growth of rabbits have been determined. Harvey et al. (1961) reported that heritability for growth rate to 21 and 56 days was relatively low. Other reports have suggested that the nonadditive genetic influence on growth of rabbits is relatively large compared to additive effects (Rollins et al., 1963; Venge, 1953; Yao and Eaton, 1954). This is generally interpreted to indicate that crosses among unrelated inbred strains or breeds should grow at a faster rate than the average of the strains or breeds crossed. Some reports have indicated that crosses among inbred strains of New Zealand rabbits were heavier at weaning than the better of the parent strains (Yao and Eaton, 1954).

Other investigators have concentrated on the effects of specific genes on growth rate and body size in rabbits (Sawin and Gow, 1967). These investigations have generally been related to dwarf or other single genes which have specific effects on body size.

In most mammals, individuality of the female has a large influence on litter size, pup survival, and subsequent litter weaning weight. Rollins et al. (1963) reported that maternal effects accounted for 28 and 25 per cent, respectively, of the variation in litter size and litter weaning weight. It was also observed that heritability of number born alive was small, around 3 per cent. This is slightly smaller than that reported by Revelle and Robison (1973) for litter size in swine; however, their discussion of genetic influence on litter size in swine could apply equally well to rabbits. In general, it has been found that animals from large litter sizes are exposed to a maternal environment that is not conducive to normal physiological development, whereas those from small litter sizes develop more rapidly than average. Therefore, selection of females from large litters would not necessarily mean that they would give birth to large litters.

Although heritability estimates for growth and litter size are small, a breeder is encouraged to apply as much selection pressure as possible to his replacement animals because of the economic importance of these traits. In other words, it is generally recommended that a breeder use desirable parental stock even though expectations for change are small.

Studies of the inheritance of milking ability of rabbits are very limited. Whether or not genetic variation is similar to that in dairy cattle cannot be ascertained. Since maternal ability of the doe includes the ability to feed her young and accounts for about 25 per cent of the variation in litter weaning weight, one would assume that differences in milk production of does do exist.

Age at puberty or maturing rate would be expected to be related to body growth. Since body growth can be influenced greatly by plane of nutrition, those rabbits on an optimum diet would be expected to have greater growth rates and reach breeding age sooner than rabbits on less optimum diets.

BREEDING SYSTEMS

Application of the laws of genetics has led to development of several types of breeding systems (selection, inbreeding, outbreeding, and crossbreeding) useful in improving domestic animals. The rabbit breeder should choose a method which is most suitable for the objectives of his production program.

INBREEDING

Inbreeding involves the mating of relatives for successive generations. The system may be well defined and very intense as brother × sister or parent × offspring mating. It may be less intense as cousin × cousin or uncle × niece. Continued inbreeding in a group of animals causes an increase in homozygous gene pairs and a decrease in heterozygous pairs. If the gene pairs for a particular character become homozygous, the genes are said to be fixed and no variation in genotype exists. When the fixed genes are desirable, improved characters are observed. If the genes are undesirable, a decline in animal type and/or performance would occur.

Intensive inbreeding is generally undesirable in commercial rabbit meat production primarily because of losses in both reproductive fitness and young survivability. Data from mouse and swine research lead one to assume that mild inbreeding with intense selection for traits of economic importance may allow a producer to attain uniformity in his animals and still maintain an economical production level. A disadvantage of intensive inbreeding is that the increase in homozygosity increases the chances of undesirable genes coming together as well as desirable genes. Chai (1969, 1970) has discussed the influence of inbreeding on performance and the use of inbred stocks of rabbits in research.

Inbreeding produces descendants which have more uniform genotypes. This method is effective with small animals in producing uniformity in inbred strains desired for research or laboratory use. Castle (1922) used inbred strains in the study of size inheritance in rabbits. There are several inbred strains of rabbits and a very large number of inbred strains of mice and rats. For mice to be considered inbred, they should result from at least twenty successive generations of brother × sister or parent × offspring matings. Strains of other species are often labeled inbred even though they have been less intensely inbred.

LINEBREEDING

Linebreeding is actually a form of inbreeding. In order to keep the genetic relationship among progeny at a desired level, related individuals must be mated. The computer is used in many large laboratories to identify matings that will provide progeny with the desired relationship level. An advantage of linebreeding is that it can lead to increased genetic uniformity within particular lines of a breed with a minimal amount of inbreeding. Producers of purebred rabbits make use of this system, and it is the one most widely used in the rabbit industry as a whole. It leads to increased genetic uniformity with less chance of undesirable characters than would be likely with intense inbreeding. The objective of linebreeding is to keep the strain of rabbits related to particular animals or their direct descendants.

The method of linebreeding from two animals is illustrated.

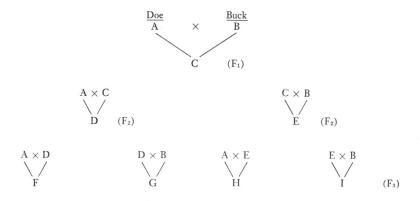

Doe A is mated to buck B to produce offspring C or the F_1 generation. (In the illustration, the left letter in each mated pair is the doe.) Doe A is mated to buck C to produce D and buck B is mated to doe C to produce E or the F_2 generation. These

F₂ generation offspring may then be mated to the original male and female. This helps keep the line related to the original selected animals and represents the closest type of linebreeding. When the original pair can no longer be bred, selected desirable breeding mates from the F_1, F_2, and F_3 generations may be used.

In most rabbit colonies, 10–15 does are maintained for each buck. A single buck, as B above, could, therefore, be used to develop several lines using different does that may or may not be related. As desirable charactertistics appear in the offspring in any line, they may be selected as breeders. Those selected may continue to be mated within the line from which they originated or, if it is desirable to linebreed less intensely, they may be mated across lines.

Another method of linebreeding with slightly less relationship is illustrated.

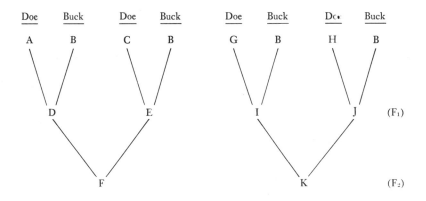

Since rabbits F and K have the same grandsire, they are as closely related to the original buck as to each of their parents. Rabbits within the F₂ generation (F and K) may be mated to produce offspring which are related but not as closely related as they would be if F and K were mated to B or to a male in the F₁ generation. Usually efforts are made to keep the line related to the female as well.

OUTBREEDING

This system involves the crossing of unrelated lines within the same breed. It can be used if a line begins to decline from excessive inbreeding since crossing tends to restore the loss that may have resulted from inbreeding. Many times linecrossing can be used to broaden the gene pools from which to begin mild inbreeding.

CROSSBREEDING

Crossbreeding is the mating of sexes from two or more different breeds. This procedure was used as one step in the development of many of the present breeds. Once the cross was made, other systems were followed to develop the breed characteristics. Crossbreeding has proven very effective in larger domestic animals produced for human food. It allows the breeder to utilize several desirable characteristics which may be present in the separate breeds since these characteristics are combined in the progeny. In addition, it increases hybrid vigor in the first generation (F_1) cross. Distinct advantages are possible with crossbreeding in larger domestic animals, and these advantages have been observed to a similar degree in rabbits (Yao and Eaton, 1954; Rollins and Casady, 1960).

Two basic types of crossbreeding are used, terminal and rotational. Terminal crossbreeding involves crossing two breeds and marketing all progeny. Replacement breeders must be obtained from other sources or must be raised by separate matings within breeds. In rotational crossbreeding, replacement females are produced within the system and assigned in a rotational manner to the next breed of sire. Much of the advantage of terminal crossbreeding is retained with this method without the problem of procuring replacements from other sources.

MANAGEMENT OF BREEDING SYSTEMS

Breeding systems must be well planned and carefully followed if they are to be effective. Objectives such as improvement of body type, of litter size, of dressing percentage, or of other characteristics should be clearly defined and reevaluated periodically. It should be recognized that more than one generation of matings may be required before specific changes or improvements can be realized. Actual time required will depend upon the objective or change sought and upon the mating system.

With any of the mating systems, selection of the most desirable foundation animals and choice of individuals to be mated are of major importance. Even for producers who follow no particular system of breeding (*random mating*), the selection of desirable breeders is important. Selection should be made on the basis of desirable breed type of the individual and desirable traits plus production records of the ancestors. Guidelines for choosing a breed are included in chapter 2 and procedures for selection and culling are in chapter 9.

Rabbits for foundation breeding stock, whether purchased or produced as replacements, should be selected from those which have been linebred for several generations. Many of the animal's characteristics will have been genetically fixed, and there will be less chance of transmitting undesirable characteristics. The mating of unrelated rabbits, even though they are of the same breed, may lead to progeny of poor quality.

Since animals tend to transmit their characteristics to the offspring, those with the most desirable traits should be selected. Even though breeders are carefully chosen from the best of those available, it must be recognized that they will not be perfect and that they will possess some undesirable traits or weaknesses. Any two potential breeders which have the same weakness should not be mated. Those which have different weaknesses may be mated with less chance that the undesirable character will be transmitted. Any rabbits which exhibit poor breed characteristics or are otherwise inferior, even though from good parents, should not be mated. Occasionally, producers will breed inferior rabbits simply because their parents were desirable, but this is a poor practice. Since 1 male is normally maintained for each 10–15 breeding females, and his influence distributed more widely than that of the female, it follows that the best available males should be used in any mating system.

REFERENCES

Castle, W. E. 1922. Genetic studies of rabbits and rats. Carnegie Inst. Wash. Pub. 320: 1–57.

Castle, W. E. 1924. On the occurrence in rabbits of linkage in inheritance between albinism and brown pigmentation. Proc. Nat. Acad. Sci. U.S. 10: 486–88.

Castle, W. E. 1940. *Mammalian Genetics.* Harvard Univ. Press: Cambridge, Massachusetts.

Chai, C. K. 1969. Effect of inbreeding rabbits. Inbred lines, discrete characters, breeding performance and mortality. J. Hered. 60: 64–70.

Chai, C. K. 1969. Inbred rabbits for research. Lab. Management 7: 43–44.

Chai, C. K. 1970. Effect of inbreeding in rabbits. Skeletal variations and malformations. J. Hered. 61: 3–8.

Chai, C. K., and K. H. Degenhardt. 1962. Developmental anomalies in inbred rabbits. J. Hered. 53: 174–8⌁.

Cohen, C. 1962. Blood groups in rabbits. Ann. N.Y. Acad. Sci. 97: 26–36.

Crary, D. D., and P. B. Sawin. 1960. Genetic differences in growth rate and maturation of rabbits. Growth 24: 111–30.

Falconer, D. S. 1960. *Introduction to Quantitative Genetics.* Ronald Press: New York.

Fox, R. R. 1974. Taxonomy and genetics. In *Biology of the Laboratory Rabbit*, ed. S. H. Weisbroth, R. E. Flatt, and A. L. Kraus. Academic Press: New York.

Fox, R. R., and D. D. Crary. 1971. Hypogonadia in the rabbit. Genetic studies and morphology. J. Hered. 62: 163–69.

Fox, R. R., D. D. Crary, E. J. Babino, Jr., and L. B. Sheppard. 1969. Buphthalmia in the rabbit. J. Hered. 60: 206–12.

Grundor, A. A., W. C. Rollins, C. Stormont, and R. B. Casady. 1968. A note on differential mortality rates of young rabbits of esterase phenotypes A, AB and B. Anim. Prod. 10: 221–22.

Harvey, W. R., R. B. Casady, A. E. Suitor, and K. E. Mize. 1961. Prenatal and postnatal maternal effects on growth in rabbits. J. Anim. Sci. 20: 907 (Abs.).

Herskowitz, I. J. 1965. *Genetics.* Little, Brown and Co.: Boston, Massachusetts.

Inness, J. R. M. 1959. Inherited dysplasia of the hip joint in dogs and rabbits. Lab. Investigation 8: 1170–77.

Issa, M., G. W. Atherton, and C. E. Blank. 1968. The chromosomes of the domestic rabbit, *O. cuniculus.* Cytogenetics 7: 361–75.

Lindsey, J. K., and R. R. Fox. 1974. Inherited diseases and variations. In *Biology of the Laboratory Rabbit*, eds. S. H. Weisbroth, R. E. Flatt, and A. L. Kraus. Academic Press: New York.

Melander, Y. 1956. The chromosome complement of the rabbit. Hereditas 42: 432–35.

Niehaus, H. 1970. The importance of recessive heredity factors in rabbit breeding. (Text in German.) Kleintierzuecht Forsch. Lehre 18: 35–36.

O'Leary, J. L., P. B. Sawin, S. Luse, A. B. Harris, and L. S. Erikson. 1962. Hereditary ataxia of rabbits. Arch. Neurol. 6: 123–27.

Painter, T. S. 1926. Studies in mammalian spermatogenesis. 6. The chromosomes of the rabbit. J. Morphol. Physiol. 43: 1–43.

Pearce, L. 1960. Hereditary distal foreleg curvature in the rabbit. 1. Manifestations and course of the bowing deformity: Genetic studies. 2. Genetic and pathological aspects. J. Exp. Med. 111: 801–30.

Revelle, T. J., and O. W. Robison. 1973. An explanation for the low heritability of litter size in swine. J. Anim. Sci. 37: 668–75.

Robinson, R. 1956. A review of independent and linked segregation in the rabbit. J. Genet. 54: 358–59.

Robinson, R. 1958. Genetic studies of the rabbit. Bibliographia Genetica 17: 229–558.

Rollins, W. C., and R. B. Casady. 1960. A genetic analysis of weaning weight of fryer rabbits. J. Anim. Sci. 19: 1226 (Abs.).

Rollins, W. C., and R. B. Casady. 1967. An analysis of pre-weaning deaths in rabbits with special emphasis on enteritis and pneumonia. 2. Genetic sources of variation. Anim. Prod. 9: 93–97.

Rollins, W. C., R. B. Casady, K. Sittman, and D. B. Sittman. 1963. Genetic variance component analysis of litter size and weaning weight of New Zealand White rabbits. J. Anim. Sci. 22: 654–57.

Rouvier, R. 1970. Genetic variability of slaughter yield and anatomical composition of rabbits of three breeds. (Text in French, English summary.) Ann. Genet. Sel. Anim. 2: 235–46.

Rouvier, R. 1974. Contribution of crossings in the improvement of rearing meat rabbits. (Text in French.) Nouv. Avic. 13: 17–18.

Sawin, P. B. 1955. Recent genetics of the domestic rabbit. Advances Genet. 7: 183–226.

Sawin, P. B., and D. D. Crary. 1964. Genetics of skeletal deformities in the domestic rabbit, *Oryctolagus cuniculus*. Clinical Orthopedics 33: 71–90.

Sawin, P. B., and R. H. Curran. 1952. Genetic and physiological background of reproduction in the rabbit. J. Exp. Zool. 120: 165–201.

Sawin, P. B., and M. Gow. 1967. Morphogenic studies of the rabbit. 36. Effect of gene and genome interaction on homeotic variation. Anat. Rec. 157: 425–35.

Searle, A. G. 1968. *Comparative Genetics of Coat Colour in Mammals*. Academic Press: New York.

Venge, O. 1953. Studies of the maternal influence on the growth in rabbits. Acta Agr. Scand. 3: 243.

Watson, J. D., and F. H. C. Crick. 1953. Molecular structure of nucleic acids. A structure of deoxyribonucleic acid. Nature (London) 171: 737–38.

Yao, T. S., and O. N. Eaton. 1954. Heterosis in birth weight and slaughter weight in rabbits. Genetics 39: 667.

6. NUTRITION AND FEEDING

The efficient production of rabbits is largely dependent upon adequate and proper feeding. Feeds make up one of the major costs of animal maintenance and of meat production. The quantity of feed provided is important, but the quality or type of feed is equally or more important. Poor nutrition can result in slow growth, inefficient reproduction, and predisposition to disease.

The rabbit is a herbivorous animal, subsisting on feeds of plant origin. In the natural state, its feed would include green forages (grass or vegetable type plants) in the growing season, and hay or dry forages and seeds in the dry season. Rabbits can consume fairly large quantities of forages, and there was a time when fresh or dried forages made up most of the diet of domestic rabbits. Although they can live and reproduce on these bulky type roughage feeds, some concentrate feed is required for efficient growth and reproduction. Most of the feed presently used for rabbits in this country is a commercially prepared pelleted diet. Selection and procurement of suitable natural feeds such as grains and good quality hay is often difficult, and commercial feeds are the most practical in most situations.

In this chapter, the basic principles of nutrition will be reviewed and their application to rabbit feeding discussed. This will be followed by a survey of feed ingredients, feed composition, practical aspects of feeding, and nutrient requirements.

BASIC PRINCIPLES OF NUTRITION

The nutritionist recognizes more than 40 nutrients required by the animal body, and these are classified into five major groups: carbohydrates, fats, proteins, minerals, and vitamins.

CARBOHYDRATES AND THEIR FUNCTION

The carbohydrates include sugars, starches, and cellulose. Wheat, corn, rice, barley, other grains, and potatoes contain large amounts of the carbohydrate starch. About three-fourths of the dry weight of the plant world is composed of carbohydrates which make up the major portion of feed for animals as a group.

A condensed general classification of the nutritionally important carbohydrates follows.

Carbohydrate Classification

I. Monosaccharides	II. Disaccharides	III. Polysaccharides
A. Pentoses	A. Sucrose	A. Pentosans
B. Hexoses	B. Maltose	B. Hexosans
1. Glucose	C. Lactose	1. Dextrin
2. Fructose		2. Starch
3. Galactose		3. Glycogen
4. Mannose		4. Cellulose

The monosaccharides and disaccharides are sugars. The simple sugars (monosaccharides) occur only in very small amounts in feeds; however, glucose and fructose occur in small amounts in some fruits and in honey. Glucose, sometimes called dextrose, is also important as the sugar in blood of animals. Galactose does not occur free in nature, but when combined with the other simple sugar, glucose, it makes up the disaccharide lactose, which is present in milk. When polysaccharides are digested, they are broken down and absorbed from the intestinal tract into the blood as monosaccharides.

Disaccharides are much more abundant in nature. Sucrose is present in cane and sugar beets and is common table sugar. When digested or broken down by enzymes it yields glucose and fructose. The various sugars may be used in purified diets for rabbits, and sucrose included in such diets appears to increase palatability. Lactose is the sugar found in nature only in milk; upon digestion it yields the two simple sugars glucose and galactose. The amount of lactose in rabbit milk is low—less than one-half that in cow's milk, and about one-third that in human milk.

Maltose, composed of two molecules of glucose, is present in fermenting grains and is often called malt sugar.

Polysaccharides include starches, cellulose, and glycogen. Starch is present in large amounts in grains, potatoes, and other root crops. It is the reserve or storage material in most plants and forms the major source of carbohydrates for rabbits and many other animals.

Cellulose is also composed of glucose units, but chemically it is more complex and more difficult to break down than is starch. It is present in plants primarily as the tough, fibrous portions of stems and leaves and, together with lignin, it makes up the component of feed known as crude fiber. Ruminant animals, such as cattle and sheep which have four-compartmented stomachs, can utilize a high proportion of cellulose in the feed. Rabbits, guinea pigs, and horses which have a functional cecum can obtain energy from a portion of the cellulose ingested. The other monogastric (single-compartmented stomach) animals, such as rats, swine, and man, can utilize very little, if any, cellulose. Several studies have been conducted to determine the degree of digestion of crude fiber by rabbits. These have shown variations in the amount digested, but it appears that only about 16–18 per cent of the fiber in a mixed diet is digested by rabbits.

Carbohydrates supply energy to the body and are the major source of energy for rabbits and other plant-eating animals. After digestion and absorption into the body, carbohydrates are metabolized through a series of complex biochemical oxidation reactions releasing energy, carbon dioxide, and water.

Digestion of starch begins in the mouth with the action of the enzyme amylase secreted by the salivary glands into the saliva. However, little digestion can occur because feed is in the mouth for only a short time. Some digestion of carbohydrates occurs in the stomach but most occurs in the small intestine where the enzyme amylase is secreted from the pancreas and continues the breakdown of starch to dextrin and to maltose. This enzyme is important in herbivorous animals such as the rabbit which consumes considerable starch. It has been thought by some that amylase deficiency in young rabbits after weaning was a cause of or a factor contributing to mucoid enteritis. This, however, has not been demonstrated. The disaccharide sugars are hydrolyzed by enzymatic action to the component simple sugars. These simple sugars are absorbed through the intestinal wall into the blood and are transported by the blood to the liver. Here the galactose and fructose are converted to glucose. Some glucose is oxidized in the tissues for energy and some is converted to glycogen and stored in the liver and muscle tissues. This may later be reconverted to glucose as needed.

The capacity of the animal body to store carbohydrates is very limited. Glucose in the blood and tissues and glycogen in the liver and muscle represent less than 1 per cent of body weight. Carbohydrates are consumed, however, in large amounts, and that consumed in excess of energy needs is converted to fat and stored in the adipose tissue.

FATS AND LIPIDS AND THEIR METABOLISM

Rabbit feeds contain much less fat than carbohydrate or protein, but fat is an important constituent of the diet and of the body. The terms "fat" and "lipid" are often used interchangeably and they are related, but lipids include the fats and fat-like substances. Fats, like carbohydrates, contain only the elements carbon, hydrogen, and oxygen, but they form a different class of compounds. True fats are combinations of the alcohol glycerol and various fatty acids. There are different fatty acids, and the nature of the fatty acids present gives the fat its characteristic properties.

Fats, like carbohydrates, function mainly as a source of energy, but they contain more than twice the energy in carbohydrates or proteins. Digestion takes place primarily in the small intestine under the influence of the enzyme lipase, secreted from the pancreas and the intestine. Bile from the gall bladder is delivered by the bile duct into the upper portion of the small intestine where it serves as an emulsifying agent for fat and thus aids in its digestion. Digestion yields glycerol and fatty acids. Some glycerol and fatty acids are absorbed and some neutral fat passes into the bloodstream. Upon absorption into the bloodstream, fat is transported to the liver where further metabolism takes place and then to the various body tissues where it may be oxidized for energy.

In addition to supplying energy, fats also supply essential fatty acids and serve as carriers of fat-soluble vitamins. Rabbit diets normally contain less than 5 per cent fat, but experiments have shown that 10 per cent or more in a feed may be utilized. Weight does not normally increase, but an increase in feed efficiency occurs.

PROTEINS AND THEIR METABOLISM

Protein represents an important and expensive portion of the diet required for synthesis of body tissue and body fluids. The animal must have an adequate amount of protein in the diet, but an excess is not beneficial and could be a disadvantage economically. Rabbits are supplied protein from plant sources, and soybean meal, peanut meal, and cottonseed meal are examples of feeds high in this nutrient. The rabbit is not dependent entirely on protein concentrates for adequate protein since there is some present in grains and in grass or hay. There is more protein in the seeds of plants than in stems and leaves and more in young growing plants than in mature plants.

The rabbit body (exclusive of digestive tract contents) contains about 18 per cent protein, and on a dry, fat-free basis the amount is about 80 per cent (Table 3.2). Although protein is more concentrated in certain tissues such as the internal organs and muscle, it is present in virtually all tissues of the body, even the fatty tissues and bone.

Chemically, the proteins contain carbon, hydrogen, oxygen, and nitrogen, and some contain sulfur and phosphorus. They are made up of large numbers of amino acids chemically bound to one another, and about twenty-two different amino acids are found in natural protein.

Digestion of food protein begins in the stomach, where at a low pH (high acidity) the enzyme pepsin causes a partial hydrolysis of the large protein molecules. Digestion continues in the upper portion of the small intestine where the action of the enzyme trypsin and the various peptidases produce the component amino acids. The amino acids released are absorbed from the small intestine into the bloodstream and are transported to various tissues where synthesis of body protein occurs. In order for this synthesis to occur, it is necessary for certain specific amino acids to be present or available. Some of these acids can be synthesized within the body; others cannot and must be supplied in the diet. Those which are not synthesized or are not formed at a rate sufficient for normal growth are termed *essential* amino acids; those which may be synthesized are referred to as *nonessential*. Actually, the nonessential acids are needed by the animal, but since they are not required in the diet they are called nonessential. Approximately twenty amino acids are required by the rabbit:

Essential	*Nonessential*
Arginine	Alanine
Histidine	Cystine
Isoleucine	Tyrosine
Methionine	Aspartic acid
Phenylalanine	Glutamic acid
Threonine	Proline
Tryptophane	Hydroxyproline
Valine	Serine
Leucine	Citrulline
Lysine	
Glycine (required for rapid growth)	

When a feed protein contains all of the essential amino acids in a desirable amount and ratio, it is a high quality protein. If one or more essential amino acids is lacking or is present in very small amounts, the protein is of low quality and is utilized less effectively in building body protein. In the preparation of rabbit and other animal feeds, it is important to select ingredients which will provide an adequate amount and quality of protein. A list of the quantitative requirements for protein, amino acids, and other nutrients is included in a subsequent section.

Ruminant animals (cattle, sheep) are capable of utilizing non-protein nitrogen, such as urea, for the formation of amino acids. This results from microbial activity in the rumen. Since the rabbit is also herbivorous and some microbial fermentation occurs in the lower intestinal tract, it could be expected that rabbits might also utilize nonprotein nitrogen. Relatively few studies have been conducted to measure the value of nonprotein nitrogen for rabbits, but most have indicated essentially no utilization. A recent study (Hoover and Heitman, 1975) indicates that urea can be used to form nonessential amino acids. Additional research is needed to determine the practical value of nonprotein nitrogen for rabbits.

INORGANIC ELEMENTS (MINERALS)

Ash or mineral compounds make up about 5 per cent of the body weight of rabbits (Table 3.2). The largest proportion, by weight, of these elements is in the skeleton, but the various elements are widely distributed in soft tissues and fluids where they function in many physiological processes. Fifteen inorganic elements are required by the animal body and must be present in the feed or provided as supplements. The minerals occur in varying amounts in different feedstuffs, and when feeds are properly blended from good quality ingredients adequate minerals should be available. When feeds are known to be deficient in any element, a supplement should be included in the diet.

The minerals or inorganic elements required by animals are generally classified as microelements (also often referred to as minor elements or trace elements) and macroelements.

Macroelements are required in larger amounts than microelements.

Macroelements	Microelements
Calcium	Iron
Phosphorus	Copper
Magnesium	Cobalt
Potassium	Selenium
Sodium	Manganese
Chlorine	Iodine
Sulfur	Zinc
	Molybdenum

Function and Deficiency Symptoms of Mineral Elements

As a group, minerals perform certain functions which are summarized as follows:

They are constituents of skeletal tissue and teeth.

They are constituents of certain organic compounds.

They function in enzyme systems.

They function in acid-base balance, maintenance of osmotic pressure, and water balance.

They function in transmission of nerve impulses and activity of muscles.

Major functions of the different inorganic elements required by the body and symptoms of deficiency are included in the following discussion. Most of the symptoms indicated were produced experimentally and would not be expected with normal diets.

Calcium and *phosphorus.*—These minerals are closely related in nutrition and metabolism and are usually discussed together. Proper calcium and phosphorus nutrition is dependent upon an adequate amount of each, a desirable ratio between the two, and the presence of vitamin D, which is necessary for the utilization of the elements. The desirable ratio of calcium to phosphorus in the diet is in the range of 2:1 to 1:1, although ratios outside this range can be tolerated, especially if there is an adequate amount of each and if sufficient vitamin D is present. Calcium is present in plants largely in the vegetative portion and phosphorus in the seed. When rabbits are supplied feed made up of the leafy portion as well as the seed, adequate calcium and phosphorus should be available.

Symptoms of severe deficiency appear in the skeleton: enlarged joints, crooked legs, arched back, and beaded ribs, accompanied by painful and difficult movement. In young animals the condition is known as rickets, and in older animals it is called osteomalacia or osteoporosis. In a less severe deficiency, poor growth results.

Magnesium.—This element is related to calcium and phosphorus in metabolism such that increased intakes of the latter two increase the requirements for magnesium. The most characteristic symptom of deficiency is tetany with low blood magnesium. There is vasodilation, hyperirritability, convulsions, and sometimes death. Rabbits were used as laboratory animals in some of the early studies of magnesium deficiency.

Sodium, potassium, and *chlorine.*—These three minerals are found largely in the soft tissues and fluids of the body, where they are involved in acid-base balance, osmotic pressure relationships, and water balance.

Sulfur.—Sulfur is present in some amino acids, some vitamins, and in all body cells. It is consumed in organic nutrients, and inorganic sulfur is not utilized by animals except ruminants and poultry under certain conditions.

Iron.—This mineral is present in the body primarily as a constituent of hemoglobin in the red blood cells. As part of the heme molecule, it is necessary for the formation of hemoglobin which carries oxygen and carbon dioxide. When iron is deficient or other factors inhibit its utilization, anemia results. Many other nutritional and pathological factors may also cause anemia.

Copper.—Like iron, copper is also associated with a lack of hemoglobin. It is thought to be involved with iron absorption and with maturation of red blood cells. Copper also functions in enzyme systems and plays a role in bone formation. Anemia, bone abnormalities, and lightening of the coat color of dark animals are symptoms of deficiency. In experimental studies of copper deficiency in rabbits, a definite graying of the black hair coat was observed.

Cobalt.—This mineral is a part of and necessary for the formation of vitamin B_{12} (cyanocobalamin). Monogastric animals, including the rabbit, require preformed vitamin B_{12} and thus do not utilize elemental cobalt. Ruminant animals, whose symbiotic microorganisms in the rumen synthesize vitamin B_{12}, require dietary cobalt.

Manganese.—Necessary for growth and reproduction, this mineral also functions in several enzyme systems. When deficient in the diet of rats, it causes delayed sexual maturity and irregular ovulation. If conception occurs, young may be born weak or dead. In experimentally produced deficiency in rabbits, a decrease in bone ash, lowered breaking strength, and shortened and crooked bones have been observed.

Zinc.—Widely distributed in the body but concentrated in epidermal tissues (skin, hair, wool), zinc functions in several enzyme systems. A dietary need for zinc by rabbits has been demonstrated in experiments by Apgar (1971) and Shaw et al. (1974).

Iodine.—Iodine is required for formation of the hormone thyroxine. In a severe deficiency of iodine, the thyroid gland enlarges, resulting in the condition known as goiter. In farm animals, deficiencies result in the birth of weak or dead young, and enlargement of the gland is readily observed in the newborn. Hairlessness is a symptom of iodine deficiency in newborn pigs. Iodine is normally supplied in iodized salt.

Molybdenum.—As a nutritional factor it was first studied because of its toxic effects on grazing animals in certain parts of the world. When the intake of molybdenum is high and copper low, toxic symptoms similar to those of copper deficiency are observed. Small amounts of molybdenum are required for the functioning of certain enzymes.

Selenium.—Like molybdenum, selenium can be toxic, and early studies were concerned with its toxicity. The severe toxicity formerly observed in certain parts of this country was known as "blind staggers" or "alkali disease," and could result in death. More recent interest in selenium involves its relationship to vitamin E; it may replace that vitamin in some but not all metabolic functions. It is effective in preventing muscular dystrophy in calves and lambs, but is ineffective in rabbits.

Fluorine.—This is the third of the group of elements first studied because of their toxicity. It is a cumulative poison resulting in erosion of teeth, mottled enamel, thickened soft bones, and eventual death if sufficient quantities are consumed over a period of time. In rats, elongation of the incisor teeth similar to buck teeth in rabbits results from excessive intake of fluorine. Evidence of a requirement for fluorine is related to the beneficial effect of small amounts in preventing tooth decay.

VITAMINS

Vitamins are unrelated organic compounds or substances that occur in small amounts in many feeds and are required in small amounts by animals. About sixteen vitamins are required; they are normally obtained in the natural feed, but if this lacks a sufficient amount of one or more, they may be added.

Since vitamins are not chemically related and their functions are varied, classification is usually made on the basis of their solubility. They are generally divided into fat-soluble and water-soluble groups.

Fat Soluble	*Water Soluble*
Vitamin A	Thiamine (vitamin B_1)
Vitamin D	Riboflavin
Vitamin E (alpha-tocopherol)	Niacin (nicotinic acid)
Vitamin K	Pyridoxine (vitamin B_6)
	Pantothenic acid
	Folic acid
	Vitamin B_{12} (cyanocobalamin)
	Choline
	Biotin
	Ascorbic acid (vitamin C)

The four fat-soluble vitamins occur in nature associated with or dissolved in fat. If the fat is removed from a feed, these vitamins are also removed. In the preparation of soybean meal, peanut meal, and certain other oil seed meals, the oil is extracted with a fat solvent, and most of the fat-soluble vitamins are extracted. In a similar manner, the water-soluble vitamins are related to and affected by their solubility in water; except for vitamin C, they are often referred to as the B-complex vitamins.

Fat-soluble vitamins may be stored in the body for a considerable period of time. If there is excess intake of these vitamins, they may be stored to the extent that animals may be fed for several weeks on a diet without the vitamin and no deficiency will occur. Water-soluble vitamins are not stored and thus a daily supply is needed.

Another difference between the fat-soluble and water-soluble vitamins relates to their synthesis in the body. Microorganisms, such as bacteria living in the intestinal tract, can synthesize many of the water-soluble or B-complex vitamins. In some animals this synthesis can supply virtually all of the animal's needs for B-complex vitamins, and this capacity is well developed in the rabbit. As discussed previously, rabbits eat a portion of their feces and obtain a significant proportion of the B-complex vitamin in this way.

Function and Deficiency Symptoms of Vitamins

The different vitamins perform a wide variety of functions in the body, and it is difficult to cite general functions which apply to all. Many of them act as co-enzymes, that is, as a part of the enzyme systems. In the following outline, only the major functions and the more important deficiency symptoms will be indicated. Most of the deficiencies described were produced experimentally and would not occur when animals receive an adequate diet. Details of these conditions can be found in many textbooks and other publications on nutrition.

Vitamin A.—This vitamin exists as such only in animal tissues or products, but its precursor, carotene, is widely distributed in plant tissues. Carotene consumed in the feed is readily converted to vitamin A and is thus the source of the vitamin for rabbits and other plant-eating animals. Vitamin A is involved in the metabolic reactions of many types of cells. It is necessary for maintenance of visual purple in the eye and thus prevents night blindness. It is required for maintenance of epithelial tissues, and keratinization of these tissues results from a deficiency. Poor growth results from a deficiency and reproduction may be impaired.

Vitamin D.—It functions primarily in its relation to calcium and indirectly in its relation to phosphorus. It aids absorption of these elements and is involved with their deposition in bone. Deficiency symptoms are similar to those of calcium and phosphorus. Vitamin D is not widely distributed in nature, but animals are not dependent solely on a dietary source. Dehydrocholesterol in the body, upon irradiation by sunlight or ultraviolet light, is converted to vitamin D_3 (cholecalciferol). Irradiation of the plant sterol ergosterol produces Vitamin D_2 (ergocalciferol).

Vitamin E.—This is the original term used for the several tocopherols which exhibit vitamin E activity. Alpha-tocopherol is the most active of these compounds. In natural products, vitamin E acts as an antioxidant, and one of its functions in animals—if not the principal function—is as an antioxidant. A deficiency of vitamin E results in reproductive failure in rats, but effects upon reproduction in rabbits have not been fully evaluated. The deficiency does result in muscular dystrophy, and selenium is not effective in preventing the disease as it does in certain other species.

Vitamin K.—This vitamin is required for blood clotting. In its absence, blood fails to clot or, in a partial deficiency, clotting time is increased. The vitamin is synthesized in the intestinal tract of most animals, and a deficiency is seldom seen. In laboratory animals, the practice of coprophagy (eating feces) provides for ingestion of some of the vitamins synthesized. Menadione is a synthetic vitamin K, more active than the natural vitamin and is the form in which it is frequently added to diets.

Niacin (nicotinic acid, nicotinamid).—A deficiency of this vitamin is the cause of the classical disease pellegra in humans and blacktongue in dogs. In humans, the severe deficiency condition has been characterized by the 4 Ds—dermatitis, diarrhea, dementia, and death. In animals, loss of weight, dermatitis, vomiting, diarrhea, and anemia are common. Niacin is formed in the body from the amino acid tryptophane, so when dietary protein contains adequate tryptophane, a deficiency of niacin is not likely to occur. Corn is low in tryptophane and diets high in this grain may result in a deficiency of the amino acid and niacin. Niacin is also made available through coprophagy, but this does not meet the requirement and some dietary intake is required.

Pyridoxine (vitamin B$_6$).—This vitamin is required by rabbits and apparently intestinal synthesis and coprophagy do not provide adequate intake. Young rabbits fed a diet deficient in pyridoxine grew poorly and exhibited high mortality, skin lesions, and neurological changes (Hove and Herndon, 1957).

Choline.—Choline is a part of the phospholipid lecithin, which is actively involved in fat metabolism and is metabolically essential for building and maintaining cell structure. Accumulation of fat in the liver is a rather specific symptom of deficiency in most animals, and in rats hemorrhagic kidneys result from a deficiency. The requirement for choline is high, but the vitamin is readily synthesized in the tissues if the precursors, which are present in a normal diet, are available. Experimental deficiency of choline has been produced in rabbits, resulting in poor growth, anemia, muscular dystrophy, and death (Hove, Copeland, and Salmon, 1954; Hove et al., 1957).

Vitamin C (ascorbic acid).—This vitamin is a dietary requirement only for primates and guinea pigs. It is synthesized in the tissues by rabbits and other animals.

Thiamine, riboflavin, pantothenic acid, folic acid, and *vitamin B$_{12}$.*—These are required in the diets of most monogastric animals, but a specific dietary requirement by rabbits has not been established. Intestinal synthesis of these vitamins and the subsequent consumption through coprophagy appear to provide adequate intake. Clinical signs of biotin deficiency have been produced by feeding raw egg white which contains avidin, a protein capable of rendering the biotin unavailable.

FEED COMPOSITION AND MEASURES
OF NUTRIENT VALUE

Many different tests may be made on feeds to determine their quality and nutrient value. These may be chemical tests which measure the amount of nutrients present or tests with animals which provide information on feeding value. The composition of most feeds and feed ingredients has been determined, and the information is available in tables of feed composition. This information is used by the feed manufacturer or the person mixing his own feeds in the formulation of suitable rations. A knowledge of feed composition is also important in comparing the nutrient intake with the animal's requirement to determine if the feed is adequate.

Manufacturers make information available concerning composition of their feeds. A limited amount of information is included on the tag attached to each purchased bag of feed, but this information is incomplete and insufficient for evaluation of all nutrients.

In order to understand and evaluate feed composition data, it is desirable to have some knowledge of how the nutrients are determined and a knowledge of the terms used to describe the different nutrient components. There are more than forty nutrients, and each must be determined separately for a complete analysis. For more general use, however, an analysis termed "proximate analysis" is made. This does not include data for each nutrient, only for the major ones, and the proximate composition plus a listing of the ingredients in the feed provide a good general evaluation. The following determinations are those made in the proximate analysis, and the terms used are those listed most often in feed composition tables.

FEED COMPOSITION (PROXIMATE ANALYSIS)

Moisture

Water is present in feed (even air-dry feeds), and the amount must be determined since it affects the concentration of the other nutrients. Determination is very simple and involves drying the feed sample in an oven at 105°–110°C. The loss of weight in the sample represents moisture. Most air-dry feeds contain 8–12 per cent moisture. Fresh greens and root crops are much higher in water content than normal dry feed. Green grass, for example, may contain 60–70 per cent water; cabbage and lettuce, 80–90 per cent; and carrots, 88 per cent. The percentage of moisture subtracted from 100 gives the value for dry matter.

Fat (Ether Extract)

Since fat is soluble in ether, the usual procedure for determination is the extraction of the fat with ether. The term "ether extract" is thus often used to designate fat in feeds. In the procedure, ether is used to extract the fat from a sample, and the ether is then evaporated leaving the fat. Ether extract is often referred to as crude fat since all the ether-soluble substances are extracted along with the fat.

Protein

The analysis for protein (Kjeldahl procedure) is made by a chemical analysis for nitrogen, and the amount of nitrogen is multiplied by the factor 6.25 to calculate the protein content. Proteins contain a rather constant amount of nitrogen (16 per cent), and the factor 6.25 is obtained by dividing 100 by 16. In feed composition tables the term protein will often be followed by the formula $N \times 6.25$ which indicates the method of determination. Protein determined in this way is usually referred to as "crude protein" because in feed, there is a small amount of nitrogen which is not in the form of protein.

Ash

Ash represents the mineral or inorganic compounds. The determination is made by burning a weighed sample of feed in a furnace at about 600°C to oxidize all organic matter. The ash remaining contains minerals or inorganic compounds. The value obtained, which is usually about 4–8 per cent for most feeds, does not indicate the different individual minerals present, only the total inorganic compounds.

Crude Fiber

This component of the feed includes cellulose and lignin, the tough fibrous portion of plants. Since lignin is not utilized and relatively little cellulose can be utilized, a large amount of fiber in feed is not desirable. The analytical procedure involves use of a feed sample which has been dried and has had the fat extracted. This is boiled first in weak acid and then in weak alkali to dissolve the soluble carbohydrates and protein. The remaining filtered residue contains the fiber and ash. This is burned in a furnace, and the fiber, being organic, is oxidized so that the loss in weight represents the amount of fiber present.

Nitrogen-free Extract (NFE)

Soluble carbohydrates (starch and sugar) make up a large proportion of the feed for many animals. However, these nutrients are determined indirectly in the proximate analysis procedure. After values are determined for the other nutrients listed (including water), they are totaled and subtracted from 100. This leaves the value for nitrogen-free extract. Frequently the listing for NFE in feed tables will carry the added term "by difference," indicating the method of analysis.

OTHER FEED VALUES

Energy

A major portion of the feed consumed by animals is used for energy. Carbohydrates and fats are the chief energy sources but it can also be supplied by protein. The calorie is the unit of measure for energy and represents the amount of heat required to raise the temperature of 1 gram of water 1°C (14.5–15.5°C). For nutritional purposes, the large or kilocalorie (kcal) is used and is equal to 1,000 small calories. Energy is determined by means of a bomb calorimeter. Maximum or total energy of a feed, determined in this way, is termed *gross energy*. Animals are not as efficient as a calorimeter in making use of all the energy in feed and an accounting must be made for certain losses. Feeds are not completely digested, so when that energy in a feed which is not digested is deducted from the total or gross energy, a value for *digestible energy* is available. All the digestible energy cannot be utilized because of losses in urine and intestinal gases, so these losses are deducted from digestible energy to obtain a value for *metabolizable energy*. Metabolizable energy is that energy which is actually available to the animal. A further energy loss referred to as the heat increment must also be deducted from the metabolizable energy. This leaves *net energy* or that actually available for growth or production.

NUTRIENT DIGESTIBILITY

One of the measures of feed value which is determined for an animal is the degree of digestion of the feed nutrients. If a nutrient is not fully digested, the feed is of less value to the animal because the undigested portion cannot be utilized. The digestive percentage for each nutrient is used to calculate Total Digestible Nutrients (TDN).

In the determination of nutrient digestibility, the percentage of nutrients including protein, fat, NFE, and fiber is determined chemically by proximate analysis. A specific amount of this feed is then given to an animal, and the feces representing the feed are collected and analyzed. The amount of each nutrient in the feed less the amount excreted in the feces represents a digestion coefficient which can be calculated according to the formula:

$$\% \text{ digestibility} = \frac{\text{nutrient in feed} - \text{nutrient in feces}}{\text{amount nutrient in feed}} \times 100$$

Digestibility determined in this way is referred to as "apparent digestibility." This is necessary because there may be nutrients in fecal matter, especially protein and some fat, which are not the undigested residue. This metabolic fecal protein or fat is usually small and constant and is ignored in this conventional method of determining digestibility. Unless otherwise stated, values for digestibility refer to apparent digestibility and are the values used to calculate TDN.

The degree of nutrient digestibility in different feeds varies, and in selecting feeds their comparative digestibilities should be considered. Reports by Voris et al. (1940) and Vanschoubroek and Cloet (1968) present data for the digestibility of a number of feeds by rabbits. The average digestibility of nutrients in typical pelleted feeds has been reported to be (in per cent): dry matter, 67; protein, 73; fat, 81; NFE, 80; crude fiber, 18; and energy, 67 (Arrington and Ammerman, 1963).

TOTAL DIGESTIBLE NUTRIENTS

Feed composition tables normally include values representing the TDN, the total or sum of the digestible nutrients. To calculate this value it is necessary to determine first the nutrient composition—protein, fat, NFE, and crude fiber. Then the digestibility of each of these components is determined. The amount of each nutrient in the feed is multiplied by the digestion coefficient. In the case of fat, the value is also multiplied by 2.25 since fat contains 2.25 times as much energy as the other nutrients. The sum of these values represents the TDN of the feed. Most mixed feeds containing grains and commercial rabbit feeds contain 55–70 per cent TDN.

FEED AND NUTRIENT REQUIREMENTS
OF RABBITS

In order to provide adequate feeds, a knowledge of the requirements for each nutrient is necessary. When the requirement for any nutrient is not met, the animal may not grow or reproduce normally and may eventually die. On the other hand, supplying an excess amount of a nutrient is neither necessary nor economical. Nutritionists, feed manufacturers, and animal producers make extensive use of nutrient requirement information in research and in formulation of complete feeds.

Nutrient requirements vary with age or stage of growth, maintenance, pregnancy, and lactation. The amount of each nutrient required may be expressed as a percentage of the total diet or as the amount needed per animal per day. When the requirements are expressed as a percentage in a feed, it is easy to compare this need directly with feed composition. Unfortunately, these requirements have not been studied and established as well for rabbits as for some other animals. Although data are not complete, some information is available; this, plus experience in the use of different feeds, makes it possible to formulate good diets for rabbits. The limited research on the nutritional requirements of rabbits has been carried out by various scientists in different locations, and the results of these studies are reported in various journals. The more current summaries of information regarding requirements are published by the National Academy of Sciences. These publications are periodically up-dated. Requirements relating to rabbits are included in the current bulletin entitled "Nutrient Requirements of Rabbits" (National Research Council, 1966). Information from this publication and other sources is included in the following section and in Table 6.2.

Total Feed

Amounts of feed indicated below as the total feed required are based upon the use of complete pelleted commercial rations fed with no supplementation. Required intakes vary with age and size and whether the doe is lactating. Lactating females are full fed, and a New Zealand doe with an average size litter will consume about 100 pounds of feed during the 12 weeks from breeding to weaning. This is an average of about 1.2 pounds (544 grams) per day.

The amount of a complete pelleted ration required to maintain mature bucks and nonlactating does is less than that which they would consume if allowed free choice intake. An intake of good quality feed equal to 3.0–3.5 per cent of the body weight will maintain them in good condition with little gain or loss in weight. For the average size Dutch this would be about 90 grams or 3–3-1/2 ounces per day and for the New Zealand, 160 grams or 6 ounces. If mature rabbits are allowed free choice intake, they will consume an amount equal to about 5.5 per cent of the body weight and will gain.

Growing young either with the doe or after weaning are full fed. At weaning and shortly after, those rabbits which are similar in size to the Dutch will consume about 3–4 ounces per day and those the size of New Zealands should consume 6–8 ounces.

FEED EFFICIENCY

In evaluating animal feeds and animal performance, the efficiency of feed utilization is often calculated, usually as the amount of feed (pounds) required per unit (pounds) of body weight gained. With rabbits, the primary interest in feed efficiency relates to that required to produce fryer age animals. Since the young generally remain with the doe to market age, it is necessary to include feed for the adult. Feed consumption used in the calculation usually includes that of the doe and that of the litter from mating to weaning. In order to determine overall feed efficiency for a herd it is necessary to account for the feed of all rabbits including those not in production. Therefore, careful interpretation of feed efficiency data for production of fryer rabbits is necessary. Since does may be out of production for varying periods of time, and the number of nonproducing animals may vary, it is best for comparative purposes to calculate feed efficiency using feed consumed from breeding or from kindling to weaning. Data in Table 6.1 relating to feed efficiency of litters were obtained using feed consumed by the doe and litter from the time of breeding to weaning at 8 weeks. The number of young per litter in this study was lower than average, and with a larger number per litter, the feed efficiency should be slightly better. The overall feed efficiency for production of fryer rabbits, using a diet with 15–16 per cent protein and including feed for all animals, should be 3.5–4.0 pounds of feed per pound of weight at weaning.

After animals have been weaned, feed efficiency is calculated as pounds of feed consumed divided by pounds of body weight gained for a specified period of time. Since rabbits can be weaned earlier than 8 weeks, additional data on feed efficiency from 4 to 8 weeks are included in Table 6.1 along with values for older ages. In this study the rabbits were full fed using a commercial pelleted diet containing 16 per cent protein. New Zealand rabbits required less feed per unit gain than Dutch rabbits, and the young of both breeds required less feed per unit gain than the old.

Feed efficiency of poultry for broiler production is generally greater than feed efficiency of rabbits. In a comparative study (Bradfield and Maynard, 1957), using a rabbit diet with 20 per cent protein, it was observed that on the basis of protein and calories consumed in relation to the edible portion of meat produced, rabbits were as efficient as poultry. In another study (Cook, 1972) comparing the energy budget of the jackrabbit (a hare) with that of sheep and cattle, the jackrabbit was considerably more efficient than either of the ruminants. Based on the caloric intake, the jackrabbit was 1.82 times more efficient than the range sheep and 2.04 times as efficient as the cattle.

Evaluation of feed efficiency must take into account the type and quality of feed provided. Rabbits can utilize some roughage feeds which are less expensive than concentrates. A high roughage diet would be expected to reduce weight gain and feed efficiency, but the reduced efficiency may be offset by the lower cost.

ENERGY

Studies have not been conducted to establish the dietary energy requirements. In terms of total digestible nutrients, the amounts indicated in Table 6.2 are recommended. These values were determined in a number of feeding trials at the former United States Rabbit Experiment Station, Fontana, California. Commercial diets which supply about 4.0 kcal of gross energy per gram of feed appear to be adequate in terms of energy. The energy in rabbit diets is present primarily as soluble carbohydrates, but it is also obtained from fat, protein, and in small amounts from cellulose.

TABLE 6.1. FEED EFFICIENCY OF LITTERS WITH
DOE AND POSTWEANING

Breed	Doe and Litter[a]	Growing Young (weeks)		
		4–8	8–12	12–16
Dutch	3.8	2.7	4.6	6.6
New Zealand	3.3	2.3	3.9	6.2

a. Feed for doe and litter from breeding to 8 weeks; 5.6 young per litter.

TABLE 6.2. SUMMARY OF NUTRIENT REQUIREMENTS[a]

Nutrient	Growth[b]	Maintenance[c]	Pregnant Does	Lactating Does
Total feed, daily				
% live wt	6.0	3.3	4.1	
oz	5.0	5.3	6.5	
g	136	150	186	
Protein, %	15–16	12	15	17
TDN, %	60–65	55	58	70
Amino acids, %[d]				
Arginine	1.0			
Histidine	0.45			
Isoleucine	0.70			
Leucine	0.90			
Lysine	0.70			
Methionine + cystine	0.60			
Phenylalanine + tyrosine	0.60			
Threonine	0.5			
Tryptophane	0.15			
Valine	0.7			
Calcium, %	0.4			
Phosphorus, %	0.22			
Magnesium, mg/100 diet	30–40			
Potassium, %	0.6			
Manganese, mg/kg diet	8.5	2.5		
Carotene, μg/kg body wt	50		50	
Vitamin E, mg/kg body wt	1	1		

a. As proportion of diet except as indicated.
b. Based on 5-pound rabbit.
c. Based on 10-pound rabbit.
d. Data from Adamson and Fisher, 1973. Other values for arginine, lysine, and methionine reported by Cheeke, 1971, and Spreadbury, 1974.

FAT

Commercial rabbit diets normally contain 2–5 per cent fat. It has been shown, however, that rabbits can efficiently utilize dietary fat in amounts greater than 5 per cent (Arrington et al., 1974; Thacker, 1956). With practical diets containing up to 14 per cent fat, the growth rate is not generally increased, but the efficiency of feed utilization is improved.

PROTEIN

Most studies of protein requirements have indicated that diets containing 15 per cent total crude protein are adequate. The requirement for the very young growing rabbit and the lactating doe is higher, probably 16–17 per cent. Mature bucks and dry does may be maintained in good condition with diets containing 12–13 per cent protein. Data for amino acid requirements have been reported (Adamson and Fisher, 1973) and values appear in Table 6.2.

MINERALS

The mineral needs of rabbits are assumed to be similar to those of other animals, but specific requirements for only a few have been established. Calcium intakes of .35–.40 per cent were required for maximum bone calcification, but .22 per cent was adequate for growth (Chapin and Smith, 1967). The phosphorus requirement, based upon several measurement criteria, has been reported to be .22 per cent of the diet (Mathieu and Smith, 1961). Other minerals for which data are available are indicated in Table 6.2.

Many older publications recommend that rabbits be supplied with salt (NaCl) in addition to that supplied in the feed. Commercial pelleted feeds usually contain adequate salt and no supplement is needed. If feeds contain no salt, it should be supplied in some way and inclusion in the diet is the best method. It adds palatability and avoids the need of supplying it as salt spools or in some other form. Salt spools attached to cages are very corrosive to the metal in most climates.

VITAMINS

Requirements for the various B-complex vitamins may be partially and in some cases completely met by synthesis in the intestinal tract. Since the rabbit eats a portion of its feces (chapter 3), these vitamins are made available. The extent of synthesis of all of these B-vitamins has not been determined, but several are known to be synthesized, and it can be assumed that others are formed. It has been shown with diets deficient in pantothenic acid and riboflavin that more of these vitamins were excreted than consumed. The synthesis of biotin and folic acid was also demonstrated. Some synthesis of niacin occurs, but this is apparently not sufficient to meet the rabbit's need. A need for choline, pyridoxine, and vitamin D has been established, but the specific amounts have not been determined. Requirements for carotene and vitamin E have been established as indicated in Table 6.2. Dietary vitamin C is not required by the rabbit.

FEEDS

MANUFACTURED, COMPLETE FEEDS

Commercial, pelleted feeds presently make up the largest portion of rabbit feed used in this country. These are prepared from various plant products and by-product feeds blended to balance the intake of nutrients. Since rabbits do not like to consume a meal or powder form of diet, the mixed feed is pelleted after it is blended. This increases palatability and helps to prevent sorting and wastage. Feeds in this form purchased from commercial manufacturers are more expensive than home-grown grains or other feeds, but they are complete diets, may be fed without supplementation, and have little waste.

The average approximate nutrient composition of complete commercial diets for rabbits is shown in Table 6.3. Two different diets are indicated. The one in the left column is the most appropriate for lactating does and growing young and contains more protein and more total digestible nutrients. Feed indicated in the right column would be desirable for maintenance of mature bucks and nonlactating females.

TABLE 6.3. Approximate Composition of
Commercial Pelleted Rabbit Diets

	Growth and Lactation	Maintenance
Crude protein, %	16.8	13.6
Ether extract (fat), %	2.6	2.1
NFE, %	52	48
Crude fiber, %	14.4	20.0
Ash, %	8.0	8.0
Gross energy, kcal/g	4.04	3.9
TDN	69	52
Amino acids, %		
Arginine	1.0	.64
Cystine	.27	.19
Histidine	.40	.28
Isoleucine	.90	.70
Leucine	1.40	1.00
Lysine	.90	.66
Methionine	.30	.25
Phenylalanine	.80	.61
Threonine	.70	.47
Tryptophane	.25	.22
Valine	.90	.73
Minerals		
Calcium, %	1.30	1.10
Phosphorus, %	.50	.53
Magnesium, %	.25	.20
Sodium, %	.29	.33
Potassium, %	1.35	1.00
Chlorine, %	.40	.45
Iron, ppm	260	200
Copper, ppm	15	14
Cobalt, ppm	1.0	1.00
Manganese, ppm	48	50
Zinc, ppm	40	24
Iodine, ppm	.8	.75

TABLE 6.3–*Continued*

	Growth and Lactation	Maintenance
Vitamins		
Vitamin A, IU/g	28	26
Carotene, ppm	40	30
Vitamin D, IU/g	4.4	4.3
Vitamin E (alpha-tocopherol), ppm	60	40
Vitamin K (as menadione), ppm	.35	.50
Thiamine, ppm	4.00	3.0
Riboflavin, ppm	6.0	5.0
Niacin, ppm	33	36
Pantothenic acid, ppm	18	18
Pyridoxine, ppm	6.0	4.6
Folic acid, ppm	1.6	2.2
Vitamin B_{12}, mcg/kg	2.5	2.8
Biotin, ppm	.17	.16
Choline, ppm	1400	1100

GRAINS AND PROTEIN CONCENTRATES

Barley, oats, soft types of corn, sorghum, and other grains are readily consumed by rabbits. However, these normally do not supply sufficient protein, although moderate growth and reproduction is possible without a protein concentrate. The oil seed meals—soybean meal, peanut meal, cottonseed meal—are good sources of protein. Cottonseed meal, however, should not be used for rabbits unless it has been treated to remove the toxic substance gossypol. Since these protein sources are in meal form normally, there may be some waste, but diets can be supplied as a mixture of grains and protein supplement. It is often difficult and occasionally more expensive to obtain the separate feed ingredients for rabbits than to obtain the pelleted rations. The compositions of a number of feeds frequently used for rabbits are indicated in Table 6.4. In a study of feed preferences Dutch rabbits preferred barley and wheat to corn, and there was a slight preference for barley to wheat. Plant proteins and casein were preferred to fish and meat meal (Cheeke, 1974).

TABLE 6.4. Composition of Some Feeds and Feed Ingredients for Rabbit Diets

	Dry Matter (%)	Crude Protein (%)	Fat (%)	Kcal/g	NFE (%)	Crude Fiber (%)	Ash (%)	Calcium (%)	Phosphorus (%)	Carotene (mg/kg)	Vit. A Equiv. (IU/g)
Concentrates											
Barley, grain	89	11.6	1.9	4.08	68.2	5.0	2.4	.08	.42		
Beet pulp	91	9.1	0.6	3.8	58.7	19.0	3.6	.68	.10		
Brewer's grain	92	25.9	6.2		41.4	15.0	3.6	.27	.50		
Corn, dent, yellow grain	89	8.9	3.9	3.92	73.1	2.0	1.1	.02	.31		
Corn, gluten with bran	90	25.3	2.4	4.04	48.1	8.0	6.3	.46	.77		
Cottonseed meal	91	41.0	2.0	4.3	30.3	12.0	6.2	.16	1.20		
Buckwheat, grain	88	11.1	2.5	3.96	63.7	9.0	1.8	.11	.33		
Linseed meal	91	35.1	1.7		39.3	9.0	5.8	.40	.83		
Oats, grain	89	11.8	4.5	4.18	58.5	11.0	3.2	.10	.35		
Peanut meal	92	47.4	1.2		25.9	13.0	4.5	.20	.65		
Sorghum, milo	89	11.0	2.8	3.91	71.6	2.0	1.7	.04	.29		
Soybean, meal	90	50.9	0.8	4.2	29.7	2.8	5.6	.26	.62		
Wheat, bran	89	16.0	4.1	4.0	52.8	10.0	6.1	.14	1.17		
Wheat, grain	89	12.7	1.7	4.0	70.0	3.0	1.6	.05	.36		

Dry roughages											
Alfalfa hay											
early bloom	90	16.6	2.0	4.05	36.2	26.8	8.5	1.12	.21	114	191
midbloom	89	15.2	1.8	4.0	37.0	27.6	7.6	1.20	.20	30	50
Bermudagrass hay	91	8.1	1.8		48.1	27.0	6.1	.42	.18	117	
Clover, red, hay	88	13.1	2.5	3.9	38.8	26.4	6.9	1.41	.19	32	54
Lespedeza hay	93	14.6	3.7		40.6	28.6	5.5	1.11	.24		
Timothy hay	88	7.5	2.4	3.9	43.8	29.6	5.1	.36	.17	47	79
Greens, root crops											
Alfalfa, fresh											
full bloom	25	4.3	0.8		10.1	8.0	2.1	.39	.07		
Cabbage	12	2.6	0.2		6.3	1.2	1.4	.06	.03		
Carrots, roots	12	1.2	0.2		8.2	1.1	1.2	.05	.04	106	
Turnip, root	9	1.3	0.2		5.8	1.1	0.9	.06	.02	103	
Bermudagrass, fresh	36	4.2	0.8		18.4	9.5	3.8	.19	.08		

DRY ROUGHAGE (HAY)

Good quality grass or legume hay is a useful feed, particularly as a supplement. Good quality hay can make up a major portion of the total diet for maintenance of bucks and dry does, but growing young and lactating does require some concentrate and more protein than could be supplied by hay alone. Legume hay such as alfalfa contains more protein than the grass hays. In either case, the hay made from relatively young plants is better than that prepared from mature, dry, stemmy plants. Hay should not be relied upon for the major portion of the diet unless it is of very good quality and shows some green color.

GREENS AND ROOT CROPS

Rabbits consume grasses and root crops, and a number of years ago these made up a large portion of their diet. These can supply some nutrients including proteins, vitamins, and minerals if a variety of plants are fed, but it is very difficult to provide the total feed needs with greens. The labor cost for supplying feed in this way generally limits its use to that of a dietary supplement. Greens and root crops contain mostly water by weight and large amounts must be consumed if they are to supply the rabbit's nutrient requirements. Greens may become moldy if left in a cage for long periods, so they must be fed with care. Most garden vegetables or their leaves and many other grasses or field crops which are used for other animal feeds may be fed to rabbits. Frequently cabbage is fed, but the amount should be limited since it contains a goitrogen which can be harmful to rabbits if it is consumed in large quantities. The composition of several fresh green feeds and root crops is shown in Table 6.4. These feeds should be used as supplements only and should be fed with care. Plants which have been sprayed or dusted with insecticides should be thoroughly washed before used as feed.

FEEDING

Rabbits may be fed once, twice, or more often daily. It is doubtful that feeding more than twice daily is of any value, and with appropriate types of feeders once daily or less frequent feeding is satisfactory. Lactating does and growing young should be full fed (free choice). They will not consume more than can be effectively utilized, and efforts to restrict feed may reduce the growth rate. Feeding devices are described in chapter 8, and those feeders which hold several days supply are desirable for the doe with a litter. Feeders must be checked, however, to see that feed is being delivered and that it has not become contaminated.

Mature bucks and dry does may become too fat for efficient breeding if allowed free choice pelleted feed or grains with a high protein and energy content. It is a common and desirable practice to limit the intake for these rabbits. Medium-weight breeds such as the New Zealand and Californian can usually be kept in desirable condition by feeding 5–6 ounces of pellets daily of a feed containing 15–16 per cent protein. If a pelleted feed with lower protein and TDN is used, the amount may be increased. If hay or greens are fed, the amount of pellets may be reduced. When rabbits are fed a restricted amount, they should be observed carefully to determine that good body condition is being maintained without excessive weight.

When hay is fed it is generally left for the rabbits at all times. Racks which make the hay available but prevent waste and accumulation in the cages are desirable. Greens should be supplied in amounts that will be consumed within about 1 hour. If they are not eaten within this time, the remainder should be removed so that it does not become stale, moldy, or contaminated.

Since rabbits consume most feed at night, a time in the late afternoon is desirable for feeding and a pattern or schedule is important. Although they may not be fed in the morning, they should be checked each morning as a matter of good management. Failure to eat is a good indication of some abnormality or disease, and the animal should be carefully observed.

CREEP FEEDING

Creep feeding involves supplying a special feed to the young while they are still nursing. It is provided in a special feeder which permits the young to eat but prevents access of the doe. Creep feeds are available from some feed manufacturers. Research has shown that creep-fed rabbits grow faster, may be weaned earlier, and the doe may be re-bred at an earlier time than those fed and weaned in the usual way. Some additional cost in feed and equipment is required, and the individual producer will need to determine whether or not this method is economical for his particular operation.

PURIFIED DIETS

Research with rabbits often requires the use of purified or semi-purified diets in order to control the intake of certain nutrients. These diets are prepared from isolated or purified ingredients of known composition. Carbohydrates may be supplied as starch, dextrin, or one or more of the sugars. Cellulose is a source of fiber or roughage. Casein, isolated soybean protein, egg albumin, and other purified proteins, as well as the amino acids, may be used to provide protein. For fat, vegetable oil or purified animal fat may be selected. Fat or oil, in addition to supplying energy, reduces the dustiness or powdery nature of most purified diets, and it appears to increase palatability. Minerals and vitamins may be added either as separate compounds or as complete mixtures. Complete mixes, balanced to provide appropriate amounts of each mineral or vitamin, are available.

Many of the early purified diets resulted in poor feed intake and poor growth and reproduction even though the known nutrient requirements were included. The purified diet in Table 6.5 was fed for periods of 4 months to 2 years and promoted satisfactory growth and reproduction. One of the major problems has been poor feed consumption, for apparently the rabbit simply dislikes the taste of some purified diets and will consume very little. With the recycling of fecal matter, the rabbit can go for

TABLE 6.5. A Purified Diet for Rabbits

Ingredient	Amount (%)
Isolated soy protein	20.0
Purified cellulose	16.0
Corn oil	5.0
Mineral mix[a]	6.6
Vitamin mix[b]	0.2
Choline chloride (70%)	0.1
Antioxidant	0.025
DL-methionine	0.2
Alpha-tocopherol acetate	50 IU/kg
Glucose monohydrate	15.0
Corn dextrin	5.0
Corn starch	27.4
Water (for pelleting)	5.0

Source: Gaman, Fisher, and Feigenbaum, 1970.
a. Composition in mg/kg: $CoCl_2 \cdot 6H_2O$, 3.5; $CuSO_4 \cdot 5H_2O$, 34.6; $MnSO_4 \cdot H_2O$, 81.1; $ZnSO_4$, 169; $FeC_6H_5O_4 \cdot 14H_2O$, 706.3; $(NH_4)_6Mo_7O_{24} \cdot 4H_2O$, 22.7; in g/kg: K_2HPO_4, 10; $KHCO_3$, 10; $NaHCO_3$, 8; NaCl, 5; $CaCO_3$, 12.5; $CaHPO_4$, 10.
b. Composition in mg/kg: Thiamine HCl, 25; riboflavin, 16; Ca pantothenate, 20; pyridoxine HCl, 6; biotin, 0.6; folic acid, 4; menadione, 5; vitamin B_{12}, 0.02; ascorbic acid, 250; niacin, 150; vitamin A, 10,000 IU; vitamin D_3, 600 IU; alpha-tocopherol acetate, 10 IU.

several days with little food and little apparent hunger. Sugar and molasses added to the diet tend to increase consumption; apparently, the sweet taste increases palatability. Rabbits do not like to eat a finely ground or meal type diet and pelleting such diets tends to increase consumption. Pelleting also aids in preventing waste and the sorting of ingredients.

REFERENCES

Adamson, I., and H. Fisher. 1971. The amino acid requirements of the growing rabbit: Qualitative needs. Nutr. Report International 4: 59–64.

Adamson, I., and H. Fisher. 1973. Amino acid requirement of the growing rabbit: An estimate of quantitative needs. J. Nutr. 103: 1306–10.

Aitken, F. C., and W. K. Wilson. 1962. Rabbit feeding for meat and fur. 2d ed. Tech. Comm. 12, Comm. Bur. Anim. Nutr., Bucksburn: Aberdeen, Scotland.

Apgar, J. 1971. Effect of a low zinc diet during gestation on reproduction in the rabbit. J. Anim. Sci. 33: 1255–58.

Arrington, L. R. 1969. Purified diets for laboratory animals. Lab. Anim. Dig. 5: 3–6.

Arrington, L. R., and C. B. Ammerman, 1963. Digestibility of nutrients by rabbits. Quart. J. Fla. Acad. Sci. 26: 275–79.

Arrington, L. R., J. K. Platt, and D. E. Franke. 1974. Fat utilization by rabbits. J. Anim. Sci. 38: 76–80.

Bradfield, R. B., and L. A. Maynard. 1957. The protein and calorie efficiency of rabbits. Brit. J. Nutr. 12: 13–18.

Casady, R. B., R. A. Damon, and A. E. Suitor. 1961. Effect of supplementary lysine and methionine on enteritis mortality, growth and feed efficiency in young rabbits. J. Nutr. 74: 120–24.

Casady, R. B., K. W. Hagen, and K. Sittman. 1964. Effects of high level antibiotic supplementation in the ration on growth and enteritis in young domestic rabbits. J. Anim. Sci. 23: 477–80.

Casady, R. B., T. B. Kinney, Jr., and K. E. Mize. 1965. Further studies of degossypolized cottonseed meal as a source of plant protein in rabbit feeds. J. Am. Oil Chem. Soc. 42: 656–57.

Casady, R. B., D. O. Everson, W. R. Harvey, and A. E. Suitor. 1962. Degossypolized cottonseed meal as a source of protein in rabbit feeds. J. Nutr. 76: 69–72.

Casady, R. B., K. W. Hagen, J. E. Bertrand, and H. G. Thomas. 1964. Effect of zinc bacitracin on the incidence of enteritis and growth in young rabbits. Clin. Med. 71: 871–75.

Chapin, R. E., and S. E. Smith. 1967. Calcium requirement of growing rabbits. J. Anim. Sci. 26: 67–71.

Cheeke, P. R. 1971. Arginine, lysine and methionine needs of the growing rabbit. Nutr. Report International 3: 123–28.

Cheeke, P. R. 1974. Evaluation of alfalfa protein concentrate as a protein source for rabbits. Nutr. Report International 9: 267–72.

Cheeke, P. R. 1974. Feed preferences of adult male Dutch rabbits. Lab. Anim. Sci. 24: 601–4.

Cheeke, P. R., and J. W. Amberg. 1972. Protein nutrition of the rabbit. Nutr. Report International 5: 259–66.

Cheeke, P. R., and J. W. Amberg. 1973. Comparative calcium excretion by rats and rabbits. J. Anim. Sci. 37: 450–53.

Colin, M., G. Arkhurst, and F. Lebas. 1973. Effects of methionine addition to the diet on growth performances in the rabbit. (Text in French.) Ann. Zootech. 22: 485–91.

Cook, C. W. 1972. Energy budget for rabbits compared to cattle and sheep. Range Science Department, Science Series 13. Colorado State Univ.: Ft. Collins.

Fox, R. R., and D. Guthrie. 1968. The value of creep feeding for laboratory rabbits. Lab. Anim. Care 18: 34–38.

Gaman, E., H. Fisher, and A. S. Feigenbaum. 1970. An adequate purified diet for rabbits of all ages. Nutr. Report International 1: 35–48.

Hoover, W. H., and R. N. Heitmann. 1972. Effects of dietary fiber levels on weight gain, cecal volume and volatile fatty acid production in rabbits. J. Nutr. 102: 375–79.

Hoover, W. H., and R. N. Heitmann. 1975. Cecal nitrogen metabolism and amino acid absorption in the rabbit. J. Nutr. 105: 245–52.

Hove, E. L., and D. L. Copeland. 1954. Progressive muscular dystrophy in rabbits. J. Nutr. 53: 391–405.

Hove, E. L., and P. L. Harris. 1947. Relative activity of the tocopherols in curing muscular dystrophy in rabbits. J. Nutr. 33: 95–106.

Hove, E. L., and J. F. Herndon. 1955. Potassium deficiency in the rabbit as a cause of muscular dystrophy. J. Nutr. 55: 363–73.

Hove, E. L., and J. F. Herndon. 1957. Growth of rabbits on purified diets. J. Nutr. 63: 193–99.

Hove, E. L., and J. F. Herndon. 1957. Vitamin B_6 deficiency in rabbits. J. Nutr. 61: 127–36.

Hove, E. L., D. H. Copeland, and W. D. Salmon. 1954. Choline deficiency in the rabbit. J. Nutr. 53: 377–88.

Hove, E. L., D. H. Copeland, J. F. Herndon, and W. D. Salmon. 1957. Further studies on choline deficiency and muscular dystrophy in rabbits. J. Nutr. 63: 289–99.

Huang, T. C., H. E. Ulrich, and C. M. McCay. 1954. Antibiotics, growth, food utilization and the use of chromic oxide in studies with rabbits. J. Nutr. 54: 621–30.

Hunt, C. E., and D. D. Harrington. 1974. Nutrition and nutritional diseases of the rabbit. In *The Biology of the Laboratory Rabbit*, eds. S. H. Weisbroth, R. E. Flatt, and A. L. Kraus. Academic Press: New York.

Ingalls, J. R., J. W. Thomas, and M. B. Tesar. 1965. Comparison of responses to various forages by sheep, rabbits and heifers. J. Anim. Sci. 24: 1165–68.

Jenkins, K. J., M. Hidiroglou, R. R. Mackay, and J. G. Proulx. 1969. Influence of selenium and linoleic acid on the development of nutritional muscular dystrophy in beef calves, lambs and rabbits. Can. J. Anim. Sci. 50: 137–46.

Kennedy, L. G., and T. V. Hershberger. 1974. Protein quality for the nonruminant herbivore. J. Anim. Sci. 39: 506–11.

King, J. O. L. 1967. The continuous feeding of two antibiotics to growing rabbits. Brit. Vet. J. 123: 453–58.

King, J. O. L. 1971. Urea as a protein supplement for growing rabbits. Brit. Vet. J. 127: 523–27.

King, J. O. L. 1974. Effects of feeding virginiamycin on the fertility of rabbit does and the development of young rabbits. Vet. Rec. 94: 290–92.

King, J. O. L. 1974. The effects of pelleting rations with and without an antibiotic on the growth rate of rabbits. Vet. Rec. 94: 586–88.

Lamming, G. E., G. W. Salisbury, R. L. Hays, and K. A. Kendall. 1954. The effect of incipient vitamin A deficiency on reproduction in the rabbit. 1. Decidua, ova and fertilization. J. Nutr. 52: 217–25.

Lamming, G. E., G. W. Salisbury, R. L. Hays, and K. A. Kendall. 1954. The effect of incipient vitamin A deficiency on reproduction in the rabbit. 2. Embryonic and fetal development. J. Nutr. 52: 227–40.

Lawrence, J. M., and J. McGinnis. 1952. The effect of Terramycin on the growth of rabbits. Arch. Biochem. and Biophys. 37: 164–66.

McWard, G. W., L. B. Nicholson, and B. R. Poulton. 1967. Arginine requirement of the young rabbit. J. Nutr. 92: 118–20.

Mathieu, L. G., and S. E. Smith. 1961. Phosphorus requirement of growing rabbits. J. Anim. Sci. 20: 510–13.

National Research Council, National Academy of Sciences. 1966. Nutrient requirements of rabbits. Publication 1194. NAS Printing and Publishing Office: Washington, D.C.

Olcese, O., and P. B. Pearson. 1948. Value of urea in the diet of rabbits. Proc. Soc. Exp. Biol. Med. 69: 377–79.

Olcese, O., P. B. Pearson, and B. S. Schweigert. 1948. The synthesis of certain B-vitamins by the rabbit. J. Nutr. 35: 577–89.

Olcese, O., P. B. Pearson, and P. S. Sparks. 1949. Intestinal synthesis of niacin and the metabolic interrelationship of tryptophan and niacin in the rabbit. J. Nutr. 39: 93–105.

Payne, A. S., E. Donefer, and R. D. Baker. 1972. Effects of dietary vitamin A on growth and reproduction in rabbits. Can. J. Anim. Sci. 52: 125–36.

Schlolaut, W., and K. Lange. 1973. Effect of flavomycin on the fattening and slaughter characteristics of young rabbits for the meat industry. (Text in German.) Arch. Gefluegelk. 37: 69–71.

Schlolaut, W., and K. Lange. 1973. Influence of methionine on growth and wool production of rabbits. (Text in German.) Arch. Gefluegelk. 37: 208–12.

Shaw, N. A., H. C. Dickey, H. H. Brugman, D. L. Blamberg, and J. F. Witter. 1974. Zinc deficiency in female rabbits. Lab. Anim. 8: 1–7.

Slade, L. M., and H. F. Hintz. 1969. Comparison of digestion in horses, ponies, rabbits and guinea pigs. J. Anim. Sci. 28: 842–43.

Spreadbury, D. 1974. Protein and amino acid requirements of the growing meat rabbit. Proc. Nutr. Soc. 33: 56A.

Thacker, E. J. 1956. The dietary fat level in the nutrition of the rabbit. J. Nutr. 58: 243–49.

Thacker, E. J. 1959. Effect of a physiological cation-anion imbalance on the growth and mineral nutrition of rabbits. J. Nutr. 69: 28–32.

Vanschoubroek, F., and G. Cloet. 1968. The feeding value of concentrates in the rabbit. World Review of Anim. Prod. 4: 70–76.

Voris, L., L. F. Marcy, E. J. Thacker, and W. W. Wainio. 1940. Digestible nutrients of feeding stuffs for the domestic rabbit. J. Agr. Res. 61: 673–84.

Wooley, J. G. 1954. Growth of three to four week-old rabbits fed purified and stock rations. J. Nutr. 52: 39–50.

Wooley, J. G., and O. Michelsen. 1954. Effect of potassium, sodium or calcium on the growth of young rabbits fed purified diets containing different levels of fat or protein. J. Nutr. 52: 591–600.

7. DISEASES AND DISEASE CONTROL

Rabbits are subject to many of the same types of diseases and abnormalities that affect other animals. Disease or illness is important because of the danger of death and because of economic losses resulting from reduced animal performance. In some diseases, the only clinical sign or symptom observable is failure to grow and perform normally or failure to reproduce efficiently. Economic loss from these in terms of overall animal production can equal the loss resulting from death. Thus, the rabbit producer must observe his animals carefully and regularly for evidence of any abnormality which might suggest an infection.

The term "disease" is used here in the broad sense of various illnesses, disorders, or ailments which may cause poor performance, sickness, other abnormality, or death. Disease states may result from infection by microorganisms and parasites (infectious diseases) or from injury, poison, and functional or metabolic disorders (noninfectious diseases). Rabbits may be affected by both classes, but the infectious diseases are of more concern.

INFECTIOUS DISEASES

An infectious disease is caused by any of the following agents:

Bacteria	Protozoa
Viruses	Internal parasites
Fungi	External parasites

Such diseases may be highly contagious, mildly contagious, or noncontagious. The infective agents are often referred to as pathogenic organisms, pathogenic agents, or pathogens. Many types of microorganisms associated with animals, such as those normally living in the intestinal tract, are not harmful. The types of organisms which can cause disease are indicated below.

BACTERIA

Many different species of bacteria are responsible for a large number of infectious diseases, including respiratory infections (snuffles) and abscesses in rabbits. Bacteria are single-celled, microscopic organisms, most of which can be grown or cultured on artificial media in the laboratory. This characteristic makes laboratory identification possible and is important in disease diagnosis. Many pathogenic bacteria produce toxins and enzymes which enable them to invade healthy tissues and cause disease. Some grow inside cells and are difficult to eliminate, causing chronic illnesses. Others grow outside cells and are more susceptible to antibiotic therapy. Bacteria usually multiply locally at their site of invasion and spread through the lymphatics or vascular system to other parts of the body. If growth is unchecked, they may eventually invade the bloodstream (bacteremia) and spread to all body tissues. Death usually follows shortly. The judicious use of antibiotics which kill or delay growth of susceptible bacteria will hold the disease in check so that the defense mechanisms of the host may act.

VIRUSES

Viral infections are caused by agents or particles which are smaller than bacteria and cannot live or reproduce outside of living cells. However, they can be grown in the laboratory in tissue cultures and can be identified by complex serological methods. Antibotics and drugs are generally not effective against viruses so treatment of a viral infection must be by indirect means. Vaccines which can immunize an animal against certain viral infections are available. Examples of viral diseases are rabbit pox and myxomatosis in wild rabbits.

Viruses redirect the energies of the cell toward replication of new virus. Thus, the cells do not perform their normal function. Many viruses rupture the host cell after replication. Some alter genetic growth patterns of the cell, causing it to reproduce rapidly as a tumor (rabbit oral papillomatosis).

FUNGI

Fungal or mycotic infections are caused by organisms which include the molds and yeasts. Ringworm appears as a lesion and is caused by fungi. Fungal infections may be external or internal, but the external is more common. Many fungi form spores (protected "seed" or reproductive units) which are very resistant to destruction by heat or chemicals.

PROTOZOA

These unicellular organisms are more complex in structure and function than bacteria or fungi. They cause damage by feeding on tissue cells and fluids or by growing and reproducing within cells. Coccidiosis is a common protozoan infection in rabbits.

PARASITES

These organisms derive their sustenance from another living organism. In this sense, microorganisms (bacteria, etc.) are parasites as well as the larger organisms. The term "parasites" generally refers, however, to the larger multicellular organisms living on or in the body. Parasites may affect growth, performance, and reproduction, and may cause death. Mild infestations may go undetected, but heavy infestations, especially when combined with poor nutrition or other disease states, can cause severe damage and death. They are divided into two classes: *endoparasites*, which live internally in the intestines and other tissues, and *ectoparasites*, which occur externally on the skin and hair. Internal parasites cause tissue damage and blood loss and may produce substances toxic to the host animal. The more common animal parasites are grouped in the following phyla and classes:

Internal (Endoparasites)
Protozoa—coccidia, amoeba, malarial organisms
Platyhelminthes—flatworms
   Trematoda—flukes
   Cestoda—tapeworms
Nemathelminthes—roundworms
   Nematoda—large and small roundworms, hookworms, pinworms

External (Ectoparasites)
Arthropoda
   Arachnida—mites and ticks
   Insecta—lice and fleas

Some arthropoda (botfly, blowfly) are internal parasites in certain stages of the life cycle.

NONINFECTIOUS DISEASES

Noninfectious diseases are not contagious, but are important to the rabbit producer, because they can result in death losses, cause poor performance in animals, and may predispose rabbits to infectious diseases. The noninfectious classification includes the following types of disorders: nutritional deficiencies, metabolic or functional disorders, genetic abnormalities, toxic substances or poisons, and injury.

The lack of specific essential dietary components over a long period of time can result in disorders termed nutritional diseases. In humans, a deficiency of the vitamin niacin causes pellagra and a deficiency of thiamine causes beriberi. Lack of vitamin C can cause scurvy in guinea pigs and humans. Deficiencies of calcium, phosphorus, and vitamin D can cause rickets in the young animals of many species. In rabbits, a deficiency of vitamin E and potassium causes muscular dystrophy. A deficiency of vitamin A has been shown to result in hydrocephalus and poor growth and reproduction. Anemia results from a lack of iron and copper. Manganese deficiency causes crooked legs and other skeletal abnormalities in rabbits. Other nutrient deficiencies have been produced experimentally, but if rabbits are fed adequate diets these deficiencies will not occur (chapter 6).

Metabolic disorders, such as abnormal functioning of endocrine glands, can cause serious problems in animals. Diabetes mellitus, for example, results from a deficiency of the hormone insulin. Diabetes insipidus, a hormonal deficiency of the pituitary gland, has been diagnosed in the rabbit, though, in general, rabbits seldom suffer from metabolic disorders.

Genetic abnormalities can result in problems with the young which may seldom be obvious. Genetically abnormal offspring frequently do not survive until birth and often do not live if born. Buck teeth (malocclusion), a serious problem in rabbits, is attributed to a genetic factor, and animals affected in this manner should not be bred since the characteristic may be transmitted to the offspring.

Abnormalities can result from injury, accidents, or toxic substances. Rough or sharp sections of a cage floor, for example, can contribute to the development of sore hocks. Occasionally a back injury may result from improper handling. Poisons or toxic substances which may accidentally contaminate feed or water or come in contact with rabbits may cause illness or death. Since these are preventable, it is obvious that good management is important.

DISEASE TRANSMISSION

Contagious diseases are those which may spread from one animal to another. The pathogenic agent may be transferred to another animal of the same species, to one of another species, and in some cases from animals to man. These infectious diseases which may affect both man and animals are referred to as *zoonoses*. Examples of rabbit zoonotic diseases are tularemia (rabbit fever), pseudotuberculosis, and listeriosis. The manner in which the pathogenic organisms are spread and enter a new host are often indirect and complex. Many of the methods of transmission are known so that, with the application of good management and sanitation, the spread of disease can be minimized. The most common means of transmission follow.

DIRECT CONTACT

When animals are housed together or can make direct contact, organisms may be transferred from the diseased tissue of an infected animal to the healthy tissue of another. Rabbit syphilis is transmitted on contact during breeding.

AIRBORNE (AEROSOL) TRANSFER

Most pathogenic microorganisms cannot live long or spread far in air, but they can be readily carried by minute droplets of moisture (aerosols). Aerosols are formed by sneezing or coughing, so when animals are housed close together the transmission of viable organisms is easily possible. Rabbit snuffles spreads this way.

FOMITES

Fomites are inanimate objects which harbor organisms in a way that permits transmission by means of contact with the object. Any number of different items of equipment could act as a fomite. Materials which can absorb water and remain moist are more effective in harboring live organisms than are clean, dry objects. Feeding and watering equipment, restraining boxes, nest boxes, etc., all have the potential for spreading disease by this method, and the need for proper sanitation is evident.

VECTORS

The term "vector" means carrier and in transmission of disease refers to an animal, usually an arthopod, which carries the infective organisms from one animal to another. In some cases, the organism is simply carried by the vector (mechanical vector); in others, the organism undergoes a portion of the life cycle within the vector (biological vector). Transmission of malaria by the mosquito is an example of disease spread by a biological vector. Myxomatosis ("mosquito disease") is a viral disease of wild rabbits and is spread by mosquitoes.

CONTAMINATED FEED OR WATER (ORAL)

Infection from feed and water is not common; but feeding and watering equipment as well as the feed and water can become contaminated and lead to outbreaks of disease. Whenever there is doubt about the purity of a water supply, the water should be tested and chlorinated if necessary.

FECAL TRANSMISSION

Infective organisms and eggs from parasites may be discharged in fecal matter and may re-enter the same or another animal. Coccidia oocysts and intestinal worm eggs are transferred in this way. The desirable types of housing described in chapter 8 and effective cleaning and sanitation (chapter 9) are major factors in minimizing the spread of diseases by this method.

BODY DEFENSE AGAINST DISEASE

Although pathogenic organisms may come in contact with or enter the body of an animal, it does not necessarily mean that the animal will become infected. The healthy animal has effective and complex defense mechanisms against disease, and in many cases the infective agents are destroyed before a disease can appear.

The skin and mucous membranes present a first line of defense, acting as mechanical barriers to infectious agents. Some of the body secretions contain a protein, lysozyme, which has antibacterial properties, and the high acidity of the gastric juice in the stomach depresses some bacterial growth. White blood cells are capable of destroying certain pathogenic organisms, and they play a major role in eliminating the invading microbial agents. Infection also stimulates an immune response in the animal, resulting in the production of antibodies which protect against further infection by neutralizing toxins and enzymes produced by the microorganisms, inhibiting their ability to infect new cells, and making them more susceptible to phagocytosis (ingestion) by white blood cells. Vaccination is the stimulation of antibody production by means of killed or nonvirulent microorganisms. After either a natural infection or vaccination the animal is resistant only to the disease agent to which it has been exposed. Viral infection often stimulates production of *interferon* which confers temporary resistance of healthy cells to viruses.

If the body resistance to infection is overcome and there is rapid development of a severe infection, it is termed *acute*. If the infection is mild and persists, it is termed *chronic*. Some diseases may exist in animals in a subclinical or latent state. These are mild infections which show no clinical signs or symptoms and may go undetected. Such an infection, however, may provide immunity to a later infection. The subclinical disease state in one animal may be transmitted to another in which it can become severe or clinical.

If an animal dies from a disease or the infection becomes so severe that the animal must be killed, the carcass should be incinerated or buried deeply to prevent transmission of the infective organisms.

DISEASE DIAGNOSIS AND TREATMENT

Diagnosis of a disease refers to its identification from the signs and symptoms observed. The purpose, of course, is to identify the disease and the cause so that appropriate treatment can be undertaken. Many different observations and tests may be necessary for a complete and accurate diagnosis. The observed symptoms may be adequate in some cases, whereas, in others, laboratory tests and examinations by a veterinarian or other professional person may be necessary.

Rabbits and other animals suffering from a disease exhibit some characteristics which make them appear or act differently from the healthy animal. Before it is possible to recognize the clinical signs which suggest a disease, it is obviously necessary and highly important to be thoroughly familiar with the appearance and behavior of the normal animal, and rabbit producers should be familiar with the characteristics of healthy animals of different ages.

One or more of the following clinical signs are indications of a disease or abnormality and each should be evaluated carefully:

Failure to eat
Abnormal breathing (rattling noise in chest)
Eye, nose discharge
Loss of weight
Unthriftiness (loss of condition, rough haircoat)
Diarrhea
Listlessness
Change in color of mucous membranes
Blood in excretions
Skin lesions, loss of hair
Elevated body temperature, pulse rate, or respiratory rate.

One of the first clinical indications of illness is failure to eat or drink. A full water container or food hopper can often alert one to a disease problem. The signs listed are not specific for a disease, but are indications of some illness. The symptoms observed, the order of appearance, and the combination of symptoms may be sufficient to identify the disease; however, when the outward signs are not adequate for identification, other tests should be carried out. A blood sample, fecal sample, or necropsy (post-mortem examination) may be necessary to diagnose the specific disease. A necropsy should be performed as soon as possible after death, since the tissues degenerate rapidly and examination several hours after death is of little value unless carcasses are preserved in some way. Samples may be refrigerated to delay tissue decomposition. Before a blood, fecal, or tissue sample is sent to a laboratory or to a veterinarian for study, instructions should be obtained from the veterinarian or laboratory concerning methods which should be used in collecting, handling, and preserving the sample.

Treatment should begin as soon as possible after the best diagnosis available has been accomplished. Following the initial treatment the animal should be closely observed. If there is no response, it may be assumed that the disease was incorrectly diagnosed or that the treatment being used is not effective. At the first sign of an illness which may be contagious, the animal should be isolated to minimize the spread. Personnel should not travel between healthy and diseased animals without proper precautions.

The various types of pathogenic agents are affected by different drugs and types of treatment. Most infective agents can be killed by one or more drugs, chemicals, or antibiotics, but viruses generally are not affected by these agents. Most viral infections may be treated symptomatically, that is, treated to relieve the symptoms and to improve general health, thus giving the animal a better opportunity to recover normally. Animals infected with viruses are often treated with agents capable of killing bacteria, because the viral infection may weaken and predispose the animal to bacterial disease. Vaccines are available for immunization against some viruses. Domestic rabbits are affected by few known viral infections, but the principle of treating these diseases is indicated so that it may be considered along with other general methods of treatment.

Many pathogenic bacteria can be killed by antibiotics and other drugs such as the sulfa drugs. Drugs and chemicals used to treat diseases are termed chemotherapeutic agents. Some of the antibiotics and chemical agents are specific for a particular group of microorganisms. Most antibiotics are not effective in treatment of fungal infections, in fact, they may enhance the severity of infection by inhibiting the normal bacteria which exert their own inhibitory effect on the fungus. Griseofulvin and amphotericin-B are two antibiotics which have been found useful in treatment of mycotic diseases.

Various insecticides and miticides are available for treating external parasites, and there are other drugs for the treatment of animals with internal parasites.

METHODS OF ADMINISTERING DRUGS AND TREATMENTS

The various drugs, antibiotics, and other treatments are prepared to be administered by a specific route. Instructions accompanying each chemotherapeutic agent include the method and frequency of administration and the dosage level; these should be followed carefully. Certain treatments should be administered only by a veterinarian, but some may be given by the animal producer or animal technician.

Dosages are usually listed as grams (g), milligrams (mg), cubic centimeters or milliliters (cc or ml), or number of capsules per pound or kilogram of body weight of the animal. In these cases, it is necessary to calculate the correct dosage for the animal being treated.

The common methods of administering treatments to animals, including rabbits, are:

Oral—through the mouth
Topical—applied locally to the skin
Parenteral—injected
    Subcutaneous—under the skin
    Intraperitoneal—into the abdominal cavity
    Intravenous—into a vein
    Intramuscular—into a muscle

Drugs given orally are administered as capsules or pills, and as powder or liquids added to the feed or water or substances given by a stomach tube. It is difficult to administer capsules and pills or to insert a stomach tube into rabbits. The best procedure for inserting a tube is to place a small board about 3/4 inch wide with a hole about 1/4 inch in diameter in the center between the animal's teeth to hold its mouth open. The stomach tube is then carefully passed through the hole in the board, into the esophagus, and on into the stomach. Care must be taken to avoid entry of the tube into the trachea. Some drugs may be added to the water or feed if they do not change its taste and thus discourage ingestion.

Topical treatments are applied to the skin or to the hair coat. Ointment applied to a body area, oil swabbed into the ears for treatment of ear canker, and insecticide powder applied for treatment of parasitic infestations are examples.

Parenteral injections require the use of appropriate syringes and needles. Syringes are available in many sizes with markings for doses indicated in milliliters or cubic centimeters (ml or cc). Glass syringes may be sterilized and reused or plastic disposable syringes may be purchased. The latter are sufficiently cheap to be discarded after each use. Needles of appropriate size must be selected. Needle length is indicated by inches or fractions of an inch and diameter is measured by the gauge—the larger the gauge number, the smaller the diameter. For most injections needles 3/4 inch to 1 inch long and 20-to-25 gauge are satisfactory

Subcutaneous injections may be given at different body locations, but the shoulder or flank area is usually preferred. The syringe is held almost parallel to the body and the needle quickly inserted under the skin. Intraperitoneal injections are made into the abdominal area, and care should be exercised not to puncture the intestines, bladder, or liver. Intravenous injections are generally made in the marginal ear vein. Considerable experience and practice are required in order to enter the vein properly, and the technique should be learned from a veterinarian or an animal technician. Intramuscular injections are usually given in the soft muscle of the upper rear leg. This injection is more painful to the animal than the others and only relatively small doses should be administered by this method.

It should be obvious with these methods of drug administration that appropriate animal restraint is needed; however, anesthesia is not required. The site of injection should be cleaned with alcohol or another antiseptic before the injection is made.

COMMON DISEASES

The following diseases are grouped as (a) microbial diseases—those caused by bacteria, viruses, fungi, and protozoa, (b) parasitic diseases—external and internal parasites, and (c) noninfectious and miscellaneous diseases and ailments. The order of presentation does not indicate a rank or relative importance.

MICROBIAL DISEASES

Pasteurellosis (Snuffles)

This bacterial disease is one of the most common disorders of colony-raised rabbits. The causative agent is *Pasteurella multocida*. It is contagious and considerable losses can result if it is not managed and treated properly. The typical and early clinical sign of infection is a mucus or mucopurulent nasal discharge. Sneezing and/or a rattling noise (snuffling) in breathing are also symptoms. Fur on the medial side of the front feet becomes wet and matted from the rabbit rubbing its nose. Snuffles may develop into pneumonia, but it is normally a chronic upper respiratory infection. Subcutaneous abscess formation, otitis media (wry neck), genital infection, and conjunctivitis may also be seen in association with snuffles (Belin and Banta, 1971; Hagen, 1958, 1959, 1966; Plant, 1974).

The elimination of snuffles from a colony which is heavily infected is difficult. Treatment of infected animals with an antibiotic is helpful, but the disease may recur when treatment is stopped. A more specific treatment can be used if cultures from the nasal discharge are made, the specific organism identified, and antibiotic sensitivity determined. Snuffles is difficult to eradicate because clinically normal animals carry and transmit infection, but the incidence may be reduced by culling rabbits with clinical infections and breeding only those which do not carry *Pasteurella multocida* in the nasal cavity.

Pneumonia

Pneumonia occurs in both young and adult rabbits. It is often caused by *Pasteurella multocida* as an extension of snuffles to the lung, or it may occur without involvement of the upper respiratory tract. Frequently other organisms (*Diplococcus pneumoniae, Bordetella bronchiseptica, Staphylococcus aureus, Klebsiella pneumoniae*) are involved. Drafty, damp, and unsanitary hutches are predisposing factors. Clinical signs are labored breathing, loss of appetite, and elevated temperature. At necropsy, the lungs may appear congested or be discolored with areas of necrosis and suppuration (Flatt and Dungworth, 1971).

Antibiotics are indicated for treatment and since several bacterial species may be involved, a broad-spectrum antibiotic (tetracycline, chloramphenicol) should be used. Isolation of the bacteria involved and determination of antibiotic sensitivity are recommended to determine the proper antibiotic.

Conjunctivitis

Conjunctivitis, or "weepy eye," an inflammation of the mucous membrane of the eye, may result from irritation by dust, sprays, or fumes, or it may be caused by bacterial infection. There is usually excessive lacrimation (tear formation) and the fluid runs down the cheek. Fur under the eye frequently becomes matted and may fall out. The rabbit rubs its eyes with its front feet, and the fur on the feet may also be affected.

At the first sign of irritation, the eye should be cleaned with a commercial eye-washing product. If the irritation is due to dust, dirt, or a foreign object the eye will normally clear rapidly. If inflammation persists, an eye antibiotic should be applied under the eyelids. Rabbits with snuffles frequently develop conjunctivitis because the feet are used to rub the nose and face. Unless snuffles is cured there is a constant source of infection. Bacterial eye infections do not appear to be highly contagious, but elimination of chronically affected animals should be encouraged.

Wry Neck (Otitis media)

Wry neck is characterized by the animal holding its head to one side; its eyes appear to be rolled back and upward (Fig. 7.1). In severe cases, the rabbit loses its sense of balance and may roll over in an attempt to walk. The disease is not always fatal, but it can cause loss of condition. Wry neck may be caused by a bacterial or fungal infection of the inner ear, mite infestation, or an injury, but it is usually secondary to snuffles.

Pasteurella multocida was isolated in 88 of 91 cases of otitis media (middle ear infection) studied in the domestic rabbit (Fox,

Norberg, and Myers, 1971). Infections apparently spread from the upper respiratory tract to the inner ear. Reasons for spread to the middle ear were not clear, but genetic factors, environmental stress, and chronic nature of the infection appeared to be involved.

Treatment with antibiotics for the bacterial infection, treatment to kill ear mites, or fungicidal treatment for mycotic infection should be carried out, depending upon the type of infection

Fig. 7.1. Wry neck (otitis media) in Dutch rabbit.

present. Drainage of infection through the tympanic membrane (eardrum) may help.

Rabbit Syphilis

This is a venereal disease of domestic rabbits sometimes called "vent disease" or spirochetosis. It is characterized by the appearance of small vesicles or ulcers on the external genital area which ultimately become covered with a heavy scab. In some cases, small lesions may also be found on the lips and eyelids. The disease is caused by a spirochete (*Treponema cuniculi*) found in both sexes and transmitted during mating (Lawton-Smith and Pesetsky, 1967).

The lesions often heal spontaneously, but they can be treated with penicillin. Recommended daily doses given by injection are

50,000 units for 3 days. The lesions usually heal within 10–14 days following drug therapy, and the recovered animal can be bred without danger of transmitting the infection. This disease is not transmitted to man.

Tyzzer's Disease

Tyzzer's disease was first described in rabbits in 1965 (Allen et al., 1965) and by 1969 had been recognized in commercial rabbitries in Canada and Connecticut (Van Kruiningen and Blodgett, 1971). It is not frequently seen, although a number of cases have been reported recently. The cause is a bacterium, *Bacillus piliformis*, and rabbits of all ages are affected. The disease is characterized by acute diarrhea, wasting, and death in 24–36 hours. It is difficult to diagnose because the bacteria do not grow on artificial media, but must be cultured in eggs or observed in microscopic tissue sections. On necropsy, vivid reddening of the cecum and focal necrosis of the liver are most conspicuous. Outbreaks are usually associated with increased stress or poor sanitation.

Treatment with tetracycline was effective in one outbreak, and the epizootic ended 36 hours following initial administration of the antibiotic. Other workers report no benefit from antibiotics. The best control measure is prevention of environmental conditions which lead to outbreaks.

Mastitis (Blue Breast)

This condition can develop very rapidly and cause death in 2–3 days. It normally occurs in lactating females and results from bacterial infection by a streptococcus or staphylococcus. The organisms are introduced through an injury such as a bite by the nursing young or a mammary injury from the nest box or cage. The first signs of the abnormality are reddened, swollen glands, decreased appetite, and frequent drinking. The gland may darken with streaks of dark blue color. The temperature is elevated and if it becomes as high as 106°F or above, the chances of recovery are slight.

Treatment must be started early if it is to be successful. An antibiotic such as penicillin, effective against the streptococcus or staphylococcus organism, should be used. Transfer of the young to another lactating female is not recommended since it will likely spread the disease. The young can be placed on a milk substitute if they are particularly valuable animals.

Enteritis Complex

For many years, domestic rabbits have been troubled with an intestinal problem called, among other things, enteritis, bloat, diarrhea, and scours. General clinical signs are loss of appetite, listlessness, dull eyes, rough hair coat, mortality, and other symptoms indicated below, depending upon the type of enteritis. Young prior to weaning are primarily affected, and death losses have been heavy but sporadic. Some young in a litter may be affected while others remain healthy. The disease has been studied for many years, but causative organisms have not always been identified. Originally it was thought to be a single entity, but more recent evidence indicates that the complex should be considered as separate diseases (Cowie-Whitney, 1971; Patterson and McGinnis, 1973; Pout, 1971; Vetesi and Kutas, 1973).

The various clinical signs and symptoms divide the complex into mucoid enteritis, diarrheal enteritis, and hemorrhagic enteritis.

Mucoid enteritis is characterized by a thick, gelatinous mucus which fills the intestine and is voided. Mucus droppings are profuse; the abdomen is distended with gas-filled intestines; the rabbit is dehydrated from fluid loss; and the body temperature is subnormal, 99–102°F. Diarrhea is not always seen, and hard, dry feces may be passed. The condition persists for 4–10 days. Enteritis is a misnomer for this disorder since it means inflammation of the intestine, a symptom which is not present in the mucoid type. Death may result from a combination of factors, including impaction of the intestine and loss of fluid and electrolytes. Treatment is generally unsuccessful, but mortality can be somewhat reduced by feeding antibiotics or vitamins and by replacing lost fluids and salts.

Diarrheal enteritis occurs more often than the other types, and clinical signs are excessive fluid in the bowel and a profuse watery diarrhea which lasts 1–3 days. It may be a clinical sign of several diseases including pseudotuberculosis, Tyzzer's disease, salmonellosis, and colibacillosis. Diarrheal enteritis is most likely to be caused by coccidiosis. In most of the studies on enteritis, there has been no routine screening for coccidiosis and many cases diagnosed as diarrheal enteritis could have been due to coccidiosis. Rabbit colonies which have been routinely treated for coccidiosis with sulfa drugs have a low incidence of diarrheal enteritis.

Hemorrhagic enteritis is characterized by bloody and watery fecal discharge. The incidence of this type is lower than that of the other two.

It is evident that more research is needed to determine the etiology and appropriate treatment for this disease complex. Until more information becomes available, the best preventive measures appear to be good management and sanitation, proper feeding, control of coccidiosis, and isolation of affected animals. If a bacterial agent is suspected, systemic treatment with antibiotics may be indicated. Replacement of lost fluids by administration of isotonic electrolyte solutions will increase survival rates. Measures taken to control diarrhea (antiperistaltics, intestinal adsorbents, and protectives) are helpful.

Abscesses

Abscessed lesions occasionally appear as enlargements under the skin along the jawline but may be found in other areas of the body. Abscesses may be the result of fighting or may be secondary to snuffles (*P. multocida*). Lesion cultures have shown that the causative organism is frequently *Staphylococcus aureus*. Abscesses usually rupture if given sufficient time, but it is preferable to clip the fur in the area of the abscess and lance it. Disinfection with peroxide and treatment with an antibiotic promotes healing.

Schmorl's disease (necrobacillosis) is also characterized by ulceration and abscesses of the skin. It is caused by *Fusobacterium necrophorum*, an enteric bacterium which may infect skin wounds or scratches. It usually begins on the lips or gums.

Coccidiosis

Coccidiosis, a common infection in domestic rabbits, can result in poor growth and performance and can cause death of the young. It is caused by protozoa of the genus *Eimeria*, which is carried by most rabbits. Unless there is a heavy infestation, the presence of coccidia may not be noted. Although coccidiosis is a common disease of rabbits, its economic importance is not well known. Adequate records are not available to determine whether or not losses may have occurred from coccidiosis or from another condition sometimes referred to as diarrheal enteritis.

Two types of coccidiosis, liver and intestinal, are recognized. The liver type is caused by *Eimeria steidae* and the intestinal type is usually caused by *E. perforans*, *E. magna*, *E. media*, and *E. irresidua*.

Coccidiosis affects primarily young animals. Symptoms are diarrhea, pot belly, rough hair coat, and loss of condition. If the young survive a coccidial infection or live to about 3 months of age, they may not be troubled later even though they are carriers. Infected adult does which are carriers will pass the infection to their young. Coccidia oocysts are passed from rabbits in the feces and undergo a part of the life cycle outside of the animal. They may be returned to the rabbit if any fecal matter is ingested. It is for this reason that sanitation is a major factor in controlling this disease. The coccidia released in the feces continue to develop in the moist fecal matter. If fecal matter with the coccidia is ingested, the coccidia are released in the intestine and penetrate the intestinal wall where they undergo further development. Those affecting the liver penetrate the intestinal wall, migrate to the bile duct, and grow there. In about 7–10 days the oocysts are again produced and are released in the feces, thus completing the life cycle. Intestinal cell death accompanying release or flushing of the oocysts frequently results in diarrhea that lasts for 12–24 hours.

The flotation test for coccidia is easily and rapidly carried out in the laboratory. A fecal sample (1–2 gram size) is mixed in a saturated solution (about 15 ml) of salt or sugar. The mixture is allowed to stand for 15–30 minutes or is centrifuged for a short time; the oocysts, if present, will float to the surface. A drop of the liquid from the surface is examined under the microscope. If coccidia are present, the oocysts may be readily seen. Since the life cycle of the coccidia is 7–10 days, a negative test may be obtained even though the animal is infected. Routine testing may be necessary in order to detect the presence of coccidia. Fecal samples taken after the diarrhea has passed are nearly always negative. Coccidiosis may be treated with certain sulfa drugs added to the drinking water; triple sulfa compounds are most effective in rabbits. Those with a sugar base are more palatable than others which may be bitter and cause severe reduction in water intake. Experience has shown that low dosages in the water for 2 or 3 weeks are preferable to high doses for 2 or 3 days. Sulfaquinoxaline, 0.1 per cent of feed for 14 days, is effective against liver coccidiosis.

Other Microbial Diseases

Several other microbial infections have been observed in rabbits, but they are seen less frequently than those previously indicated.

Pseudotuberculosis.—This condition is caused by *Yersinia pseudotuberculosis* and is characterized by macroscopic lesions similar to those of tuberculosis. They are observed in the parenchyma of the liver, lungs, spleen, and intestinal wall. Clinical signs in affected animals are listlessness, loss of appetite, loss of weight, and labored breathing. The disease is zoonotic, and infected animals should be destroyed.

Listeriosis.—*Listeria monocytogenes* is the cause of this bacterial infection. Most outbreaks in rabbits are associated with environmental or physiological stress. There is appetite loss and emaciation, and small white abscesses appear in the liver, spleen, and reproductive organs. The central nervous system may be affected, resulting in a twisting of the head as in wry neck. Involvement of the uterus may result in abortion. This disease also has zoonotic potential.

Myxomatosis.—This viral disease is transmitted by an arthropod vector, the principal one being the mosquito. The disease spreads rapidly, and mortality is high in the European wild rabbit and the domestic rabbit. Clinical signs are fever, labored breathing, drooping edematous ears, mucinous skin tumors, and swollen and crusty eyelids, nose, mouth, and genital organs. Internal symptoms include congested lungs, enlarged dark spleen, and congested peripheral blood vessels. Death occurs in 1–2 weeks. The disease has been reported in the western United States where it is enzootic in the wild rabbit population. In this area it is advisable to screen the rabbit quarters in order to keep the mosquito vector out.

Fibromatosis.—A virus closely related to the myxomatosis virus is the cause of this disorder. It causes subcutaneous tumors which regress after several months. The disease is more widespread than myxomatosis, but it is not a significant problem in domestic rabbit production.

Papillomatosis.—This is a viral disease in which benign tumors (papillomas) are produced. They appear on the body, where they resemble long horny warts, or in the mouth, usually on the underside of the tongue. The two forms are caused by different viruses. The growths usually regress after a few months, but skin papillomas may become malignant. These diseases are somewhat geographically restricted in incidence, oral papillomatosis occurring in the vicinity of New York and the other form west of the Mississippi River.

Tularemia (rabbit fever).—*Francisella tularensis* is the cause of this infectious and highly contagious disease of wild rabbits. The organism is infectious for many other vertebrates, including man. The disease is acute and mortality is high. Tularemia is not a problem in domestic rabbit colonies.

Ringworm.—This mycotic infection is usually caused by the fungus *Trichophyton* in the rabbit. Lesions are circular, bald, reddened patches and may appear on any area of the skin although they usually begin on the head. They spread peripherally, forming a yellow crust which usually sloughs off in about 3 weeks and is followed by the appearance of small ulcers. At first there seems to be little irritation, but later considerable scratching is observed.

Hair should be clipped from the affected area which should then be treated with a fungicide and/or systematically with griseofulvin (Hagen, 1969). Ringworm is also infectious for man, so care should be taken in the handling of infected rabbits.

PARASITIC DISEASES

Cysticercosis (Tapeworm)

Cysticercosis is parasitism of the rabbit by tapeworm cysts. The rabbit acts as an intermediate host for the dog and cat tapeworm (*Taenia pisiformis, Multiceps serialis,* and *Taenia taeniaeformis*), and infection occurs when the tapeworm eggs are consumed with the feed. The eggs develop to the larval stage in the rabbit and migrate throughout the body. On necropsy, fibrous tracks may be seen in the liver and white cysts may be attached to the viscera and liver or under the skin.

Heavy infections of tapeworm larvae cause the rabbits to appear unthrifty while light infections usually go undetected. To prevent such infestations, dogs and cats should not be allowed near rabbits.

Other internal parasites which may affect the rabbit are the protozoan *Encephalitozoon (Nosema) cuniculi,* the fluke *Dicrocoelium dendriticum,* and the nematodes *Obeliscoides strigosum, Physocephalus sexalatus, Trichostrongylus retortaeformis, Passalurus ambiguus, Trichuris leporis,* and *Protostrongylus refescens.* Infections by these parasites, except for *E. cuniculi* and *P. ambiguus,* are not common, but can occur, and diagnosis and treatment should be handled by a veterinarian.

Warbles

Warbles results from the growth under the skin of larvae from the botfly (*Cuterebra* sp.). The adult fly, which is seldom seen, deposits eggs in the hair. Upon hatching, the larvae penetrate the skin and continue to develop, causing swelling and irritation. The warbles may be observed easily as enlargements under the skin with a small hole in the center; the fur around the hole may be matted. The lesion is painful and the rabbit may lick the area.

Treatment involves lancing the skin under local anesthesia and removing the larvae or grubs. The area should be treated with an antiseptic after lancing. The larvae should not be crushed in the rabbit, since it may cause tissue damage and/or a toxic reaction. This disease can be prevented by screening to keep the botfly away from the rabbit.

Ear Canker

This parasitic infestation is a common problem in rabbits (Fig. 7.2), but it can be easily controlled. The cause is a small mite (*Psoroptes cuniculi*) which feeds on the epithelial tissues and fluids of the ear canal. This causes leakage of the tissue fluid which hardens, leaving thick crusts or scabs beneath which the mites continue to live. Considerable irritation and discomfort is caused to the rabbit; it will shake its head and attempt to scratch its ears with its hind feet. With heavy infestations the animal becomes unthrifty and loses weight. The lesion can be very easily seen, and rabbits should be observed periodically to detect ear canker before it becomes serious. Treatment is much easier in the early stages than in severe infections.

The causal mite breathes through its body and can be eliminated or killed by suffocation. Oil, such as mineral or vegetable, is effective; it coats the body surface and prevents breathing. Insecticides, such as rotenone, may be incorporated in the oil. With heavy infestation and thick scabs, the oil may not penetrate to all of the mites. One or two treatments will soon clear the scales, but some mites may remain and the canker may reappear within 8–12 weeks. Repeated treatments may be necessary. Topical antibiotics are sometimes needed to control bacteria which may invade the inflamed skin of the ear canal. When treating an infected animal, those in adjoining cages should also be treated as a precautionary measure.

Mange Mite

Rabbits occasionally may become infected with the mange mite which infects dogs (*Sarcoptes scabei*) and the mite which affects cats (*Notoedres cati*). Different parts of the body may be affected, and infestation can be suspected when rabbits scratch

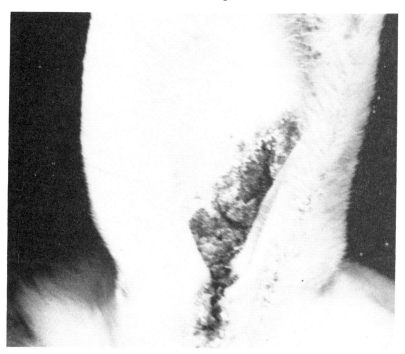

Fig. 7.2. Ear canker.

themselves frequently and there is some loss of hair. The mites burrow through the skin and are very irritating. The condition is contagious and is very difficult to eliminate, but miticide dusts properly applied can provide the necessary control.

Fur Mite

Many rabbits are infected with fur mites of the family Listrophoridae. These are endemic throughout the United States and appear on many mammals in warm weather. They are of no real economic importance to the rabbit breeder and seldom cause serious problems. Breeders of laboratory animals, however, should be very careful that rabbits sold for laboratory use are not infested. Infected animals exhibit a generalized loss of hair, and thus the disorder is frequently confused with molting.

NONINFECTIOUS DISEASES

Malocclusion (Buck Teeth)

This abnormality is characterized by excessive growth of the incisor or front teeth (Fig. 7.3). These teeth grow about 4 inches per year throughout the life span of the rabbit but are worn away in the normal process of eating. If any factor operates to prevent the teeth from wearing away normally, they may grow excessively long. The continued growth prevents proper closing of the jaws and interferes with eating. The condition is an inherited characteristic resulting from recessive genes. It occurs when both parents carry the gene and each passes the gene to the offspring. Pairing of the recessive genes results in anterior displacement forward of the jawbone so that the upper and lower incisors do not meet properly and normal wear cannot occur. Since buck teeth is an inherited characteristic the number of rabbits carrying the undesirable gene will increase in a breeding colony unless specific culling is carried out to eliminate these animals. There is no cure for this condition other than culling. Temporary treatment involves cutting away the excessive growth, using heavy scissors or wire cutters. This permits the young to eat and attain slaughter weight. The teeth will continue to grow, however, and repeated trimming may be required in 2–3 weeks.

Most cases of buck teeth are hereditary, but occasionally excessive growth appears to result from other causes. If an incisor tooth is broken, excessive growth may begin and continue. An abscess in the region of the molar teeth which prevents normal eating may also result in excessive growth of the incisors.

Malocclusion of the premolar and molar teeth (cheek teeth) may occur also, but it is observed less frequently. This type of

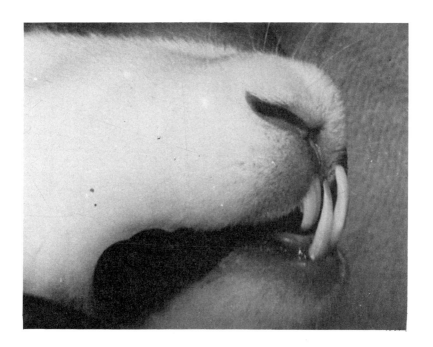

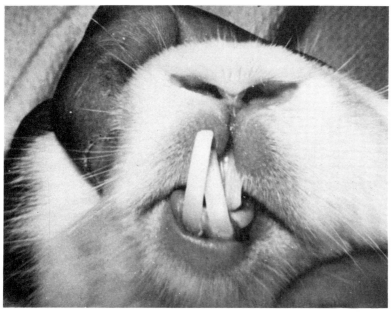

Fig. 7.3. Malocclusion (buck teeth).

malocclusion is caused by damage to the teeth resulting in improper matching of the upper and lower teeth. Since the premolars and molars grow continuously, matching of the teeth is necessary for proper wear. Sharp edges develop at the inside (lower incisors) or outside (upper incisors) tooth margins. The rabbit may be unable to chew food and saliva will drool from its mouth, giving rise to the term "slobbers," which is sometimes used to identify the condition.

Sore Hocks

The undersurface of the hind feet as well as the pads and toes of the front feet may become inflamed and ulcerated from pressure of these areas on the wire floors of the cage (Fig. 7.4). Evidence of the problem may be seen when rabbits shift their weight from one foot to another and show signs of discomfort. Lesions may be seen on the feet or on the foot pad. Mortality is not great or an immediate result, but the disorder can cause losses resulting in poor condition, inability of the doe to nurse the litter properly, and interference with breeding.

Predisposing factors which may contribute to the problem are hereditary and environmental. Sore hocks is not inherited, but predisposition to the condition may be. If the animal is inherently nervous and excitable and is active with excessive foot stamping, this may contribute to the development of sore hocks. Likewise the hair or fur on the foot pads of some animals may be thin and therefore not provide a desirable cushion for housing on the wire floors normally used in domestic rabbit cages. Larger breeds are more commonly affected. Since there is an inherent predisposition to this disease, it is obvious that rabbits with a habitual tendency toward sore hocks should not be used as breeders. Environmental factors include excess moisture, urine, or filth on the hutch floor, rough surfaces on the floor, or a floor constructed of the wrong size wire grid. Environmental factors which predispose animals to sore hocks can be corrected by housing or management procedures.

Sore hocks is usually difficult to heal. The use of dry, soft bedding material or a resting board to keep the rabbit off the

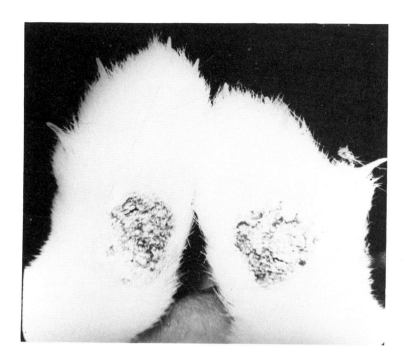

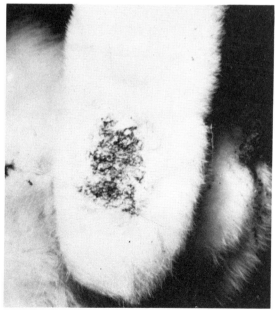

Fig. 7.4. Examples of sore hocks. Upper, front feet. Lower, rear foot.

wire floor is helpful. If the lesion becomes infected and abscessed it should be lanced and the pus removed, and the area irrigated with an antiseptic and treated with an antibiotic ointment.

Caked Mammary Glands

Caked breasts result when the milk produced is not withdrawn sufficiently from the glands. This may occur when there is loss of the litter, when the doe is a high producing mother, or when the nipples or mammary glands become sore and the doe will not allow the young to nurse. If a gland is caked only slightly, the application of camphor oil to it twice daily will usually break up the cake, and the milk may be removed manually. Usually treatment for 3–5 days is sufficient for clearing up this problem. If a doe is a heavy milk producer, however, longer treatment may be required. If the mammary gland becomes severely caked, it should be lanced, all of the caked milk removed, and the area irrigated with peroxide or another disinfectant. Treatment with an antibiotic ointment is recommended. Caked breast is often mistaken for mastitis. The condition may predispose the female to subsequent mammary infection.

Fur Block (Hair Ball)

Most rabbits ingest small amounts of hair during the normal practice of grooming. A fur block may result when a rabbit consumes large amounts of its own hair or that from another in a short period of time. The fur mixes with the stomach contents and forms a firm ball which cannot pass through the pyloric valve between the stomach and the small intestine. Fur block may be suspected when rabbits eat only small amounts of feed sporadically and when there are no other clinical signs to indicate the resulting loss of condition. It may be possible to palpate the hair ball in the stomach. It has been thought that excessive fur eating may result from too little roughage in the diet, but more recent evidence indicates that a deficiency of the amino acids methionine and cystine may be involved. Fur block is noted more often in Angora rabbits, which have long hair, than in other breeds which have short hair. Early treatment with an oral dose of mineral oil may be successful, but if the ball is too large to pass out of the stomach this treatment is not effective.

Wet Dewlap

Wet dewlap commonly occurs during warm weather in rabbits which drink from a water crock. Rabbits tend to get the dewlap (the fold of skin under the neck) into the water when drinking. This part of the body may remain continuously damp, and the fur mats and may harbor microorganisms. The area of the fur may turn green as the microorganisms grow. Removal of the wet fur by clipping and treatment of the skin with a powder for 3–4 days promotes healing. Raising the water crock 2 or 3 inches above the cage floor or using water bottles with sipper tubes aids in keeping the dewlap dry. A similar condition occurs in rabbits that lie under leaking automatic waterers. The area affected is usually the back or side, and the appearance is similar to that of a wet dewlap.

Hutch Burn

Hutch burn is often confused with rabbit syphilis or the true vent disease. It affects the external genitalia and is usually associated with wet and dirty hutches. Exposure of the genital tissues to urine splashes and fecal debris causes the membranes to become irritated and secondarily infected. Brownish crusts usually cover the area and a bleeding exudate may be present. Cages should be kept sanitary, particularly the floors, so that manure and debris are not allowed to accumulate. Affected animals should be treated topically with an antibiotic ointment to speed recovery.

Spinal Fracture

Spinal fracture results in posterior paralysis and incontinence (loss of control of urination and defecation). The injury may occur if the rabbit kicks excessively when the rear legs are not properly supported. Rabbits should always be held so that they will not kick and struggle. The injury can result from forcing a rabbit into a restraint box of insufficient size or from other types of handling which induce struggling. A rabbit with a dislocated spine usually cannot be treated and should be destroyed, although if the spinal cord has not been too severely damaged partial recovery may occur.

Heat Exhaustion (Heat Stroke)

Heat exhaustion may be caused by excessively high environmental temperatures (92°F or above) or exposure to heat and poor ventilation, which can occur in transport. Pregnant does are most often affected, but rabbits of all ages are susceptible. Young in the nest box are particularly susceptible when there is excessive bedding and little ventilation. Clinical signs are prostration, increased respiration rate, cyanosis, and evidence of blood in the discharge from the mouth and nose.

Mortality can be high unless environmental temperatures can be reduced and individual units treated as required. In buildings that may become excessively hot from heat radiated from the roof, a water sprinkler can help reduce the temperature. Rabbits suffering from heat exhaustion may be immersed in lukewarm water to reduce body temperature to the normal 101–104°F. Placing exhausted animals on wet burlap in the cage will aid cooling. Care should be exercised in transport of animals to insure that crates are adequately ventilated and that temperature in the vehicles does not become too high.

Yellow Fat

The body fat of rabbits is normally white or colorless, and the muscle tissue is light colored, making a light-colored carcass. In a few breeds, rabbits occasionally have yellow fat. Since consumers of rabbit meat are accustomed to white carcasses, the presence of yellow fat causes some to assume that the meat is undesirable. Actually the yellow fat is harmless, but the color is considered objectionable and the animals not marketable for meat. Rabbits which produce offspring with yellow fat should not be used in a breeding colony.

The yellow color results from the presence of carotenoid pigments, xanthophylls, which are fat soluble. The pigments are present in many plant materials, and most rabbits metabolize them to colorless materials. Those unable to metabolize the xanthophylls lack an enzyme, normally present in the liver, which is capable of acting on the pigment. The absence of the enzyme is an inherited factor resulting from a mutation of the dominant (Y) gene to a recessive (y), which is inherited as a complete recessive to the normal (Y). If xanthophylls are not consumed, yellow fat will not occur even though the liver enzyme is lacking.

REFERENCES

Allen, A. M., J. R. Ganaway, T. D. Moore, and R. F. Kinard. 1965. Tyzzer's disease syndrome in laboratory rabbits. Am. J. Path. 46: 859–81.

Banks, K. L., and T. B. Clarkson. 1967. Naturally occurring dermatomycosis in the rabbit. J. Am. Vet. Med. Assn. 151: 926–29.

Bedson, H. S., and M. J. Duckworth. 1963. Rabbit pox: An experimental study of the pathways of infection in rabbits. J. Path. Bact. 85: 1–20.

Belin, R. P., and R. G. Banta. 1971. Successful control of snuffles in a rabbit colony. J. Am. Vet. Med. Assn. 159: 622–23.

Boorman, G. A., and M. M. Bree. 1969. Diabetes insipidus syndrome in a rabbit. J. Am. Vet. Med. Assn. 155: 1218–20.

Cowie-Whitney, J. 1971. Some aspects of the enteritis complex of rabbits. In *Nutrition and Disease in Experimental Animals*, ed. W. D. Tavernor. Balliere, Tindall and Cassel: London.

Flatt, R. E. 1974. Bacterial diseases. In *The Biology of the Laboratory Rabbit*, eds. S. H. Weisbroth, R. E. Flatt, and A. L. Kraus. Academic Press: New York.

Flatt, R. E., and D. L. Dungworth. 1971. Enzootic pneumonia in rabbits: Microbiology and comparison with lesions experimentally produced by *Pasteurella multocida* and a chlamydial organism. Am. J. Vet. Res. 32: 627–36.

Flatt, R. E., and D. L. Dungworth. 1971. Enzootic pneumonia in rabbits: Naturally occurring lesions in lungs of apparently healthy young rabbits. Am. J. Vet. Res. 32: 621–26.

Flatt, R. E., S. H. Weisbroth, and A. L. Kraus. 1974. Metabolic, traumatic, mycotic and miscellaneous diseases of rabbits. In *The Biology of the Laboratory Rabbit*, eds. S. H. Weisbroth, R. E. Flatt, and A. L. Kraus. Academic Press: New York.

Fox, R. R., and D. D. Crary. 1971. Mandibular prognathism in the rabbit. J. Hered. 62: 23–27.

Fox, R. R., R. F. Norberg, and D. D. Myers. 1971. The relationship of *Pasteurella multocida* to otitis media in the domestic rabbit (*O. cuniculus*). Lab. Anim. Sci. 21: 45–48.

Greve, J. H. 1959. Some diseases of domestic rabbits. Mich. State Univ. Veterinarian 19: 84–89.

Hagen, K. W. 1958. Enzootic pasteurellosis in domestic rabbits. 1. Pathology and bacteriology. J. Am. Vet. Med. Assn. 133: 77–80.

Hagen, K. W. 1959. Chronic respiratory infection in the domestic rabbit. Proc. Anim. Care Panel 9: 55–60.

Hagen, K. W. 1963. Disseminated staphylococcic infection in young domestic rabbits. J. Am. Vet. Med. Assn. 142: 1421–22.

Hagen, K. W. 1966. Enzootic pasteurellosis in rabbits. 2. Strain types and methods of control. Lab. Anim. Care 16: 487–91.

Hagen, K. W. 1966. Papillomatosis in rabbits. Bull. Wildlife Disease Assn. 2: 108–10.

Hagen, K. W. 1969. Ringworm in domestic rabbits: Oral treatment with griseofulvin. Lab. Anim. Care 19: 655–68.

Jones, J. B., and D. E. Bailey. 1971. Diseases of domestic rabbits. A bibliography. Lab. Anim. 5: 207–12.

Koller, K. W. 1969. Spontaneous *Nosema cuniculi* infection in laboratory rabbits. J. Am. Vet. Med. Assn. 155: 1108–14.

Kraus, A. L. 1974. Arthropod parasites. In *The Biology of the Laboratory Rabbit*, eds. S. H. Weisbroth, R. E. Flatt, and A. L. Kraus. Academic Press: New York.

Lawton-Smith, J., and B. R. Pesetsky. 1967. The current status of *Treponema cuniculi*. A review of the literature. Brit. J. Vener. Dis. 43: 117–27.

Levine, N. D., and V. Ivens. 1972. Coccidia of the Leporidae. J. Protozool. 19: 572–81.

McDonald, R. A., and A. F. Pinheiro. 1967. Water chlorination controls *Pseudomonas aeruginosa* in a rabbitry. J. Am. Vet. Med. Assn. 151: 863–64.

Mack, R. 1962. Disorders of the digestive tract of domesticated rabbits. Vet. Bull. 32: 191–99.

Mare, C. J. 1974. Viral diseases. In *The Biology of the Laboratory Rabbit*, eds. S. H. Weisbroth, R. E. Flatt, and A. L. Kraus. Academic Press: New York.

Ostler, D. C. 1961. The diseases of broiler rabbits. Vet. Record 73: 1237–52.

Pakes, S. P. 1974. Protozoal diseases. In *The Biology of the Laboratory Rabbit*, eds. S. H. Weisbroth, R. E. Flatt, and A. L. Kraus. Academic Press: New York.

Patterson, L. T., and S. K. McGinnis. 1973. Coliform enteritis in rabbits. Ark. Farm Res. 22: 7.

Plant, J. W. 1974. Control of *Pasteurella multocida* infections in a small rabbit colony. Lab. Anim. 8: 39–40.

Pout, D. 1971. Mucoid enteritis in rabbits. Vet. Record 89: 214–16.

Ringler, D. H., and G. D. Abrams. 1970. Nutritional muscular dystrophy and neonatal mortality in a rabbit breeding colony. J. Am. Vet. Med. Assn. 157: 1928–34.

Rutherford, R. L. 1943. The life cycle of four intestinal coccidia of the domestic rabbit. J. Parasit. 29: 10–32.

Testoni, F. J. 1974. Enzootic renal nosematosis in laboratory rabbits. Aust. Vet. J. 50: 159–63.

Van Kampen, K. R. 1968. Lymphosarcoma in the rabbit. A case report and general review. Cornell Vet. 58: 121–28.

Van Kruiningen, H. J., and S. B. Blodgett. 1971. Tyzzer's disease in a Connecticut rabbitry. J. Am. Vet. Med. Assn. 158: 1205–12.

Vetesi, F., and F. Kutas. 1973. Mucoid enteritis in the rabbit associated with *Escherichia coli* changes in water, electrolyte and acid-base balance. Acta Vet. 23: 381–88.

Weisbroth, S. H., and L. Ehrman. 1967. Malocclusion in the rabbit: A model for the study of the development, pathology and inheritance of malocclusion. 1. Preliminary note. J. Hered. 58: 245–46.

Wescott, R. B. 1974. Helminth parasites. In *The Biology of the Laboratory Rabbit*, eds. S. H. Weisbroth, R. E. Flatt, and A. L. Kraus. Academic Press: New York.

Zeman, W. V., and F. G. Fielder. 1969. Dental malocclusion and overgrowth in rabbits. J. Am. Vet. Med. Assn. 155: 1115–19.

8. HOUSING, CAGING, AND EQUIPMENT

The provision of suitable housing and caging is an important aspect of the efficient production of rabbits. Improper housing and caging can be related to occurrences of disease and other abnormalities and to the discomfort of the animals. The cages or hutches in which rabbits are maintained represent their home for life. All of the life processes—eating, sleeping, reproduction, and other activities—take place in this enclosure. This type of confinement is far from the natural environment, but fortunately domestic rabbits can adapt.

Rabbit cages should be designed and constructed as more than places of confinement. Comfort of the animal, adequate space for all of the life processes, prevention of injury, features to aid in disease control, and ease of cleaning and servicing are important. Housing must protect from the extremes of heat and cold, rain, and all other adverse environmental conditions. Rabbits maintained for research and many of those produced for research are housed in buildings which have automatic temperature, humidity, and fresh air controls. In the laboratory, desirable environmental conditions for rabbits are: temperature, 68–72°F; humidity, 40–60 per cent; and 10–15 changes of air per hour. The average rabbit producer cannot expect to provide housing with complete mechanical control of the environment, and it is not practical or necessary. Knowledge of the more ideal condition, however, is desirable as a guide and a goal in an effort to provide the best housing conditions practical.

All rabbits should be housed in separate or individual cages, with the exception of the doe and her litter or young rabbits held

162

together for a brief period before marketing. Adult rabbits normally fight excessively when penned together, and efforts to house them in groups or colonies generally have not been successful. Because of the need for individual caging, the housing cost per animal is obviously greater than it would be if they could be housed in larger groups. Therefore, cages should be designed and arranged within a building to accommodate the maximum number of animals and to provide the most ease in the servicing of the cages. Many different types of housing are used and no one specific method is considered ideal. Choice of the type of housing depends on location, number of rabbits, production purposes, and other factors.

HOUSING

Although there are many different forms of housing, there are two general categories. The most widely used type is a shed (barn) or other structure fitted with cages. The second type consists of single, duplex, or multiple self-contained outside units, which are convenient when buildings are not possible, and when economy is an important factor.

An example of the first type of building is shown in Figure 8.1. The building may be of any size suitable to accommodate the herd or number of rabbits maintained. With the cages arranged as single tier units, a building having about 2000 square feet of floor space should accommodate 100 medium-weight breeding does. This would not include space required for replacements being raised or others being held. In warm climates this structure may consist primarily of a shed which protects from rain and direct sun. Various construction materials are used, including wood, aluminum, and steel. The building floor is an important consideration. Most commercial rabbitries have concrete aisles, and the area directly under the cages usually consists of a drainage bed made of tile or gravel from which fecal droppings are removed periodically. Sealed floors, made of concrete and sloped for drainage, are used when the rabbit cage housing utilizes litter pans such as in research institutions.

Fig. 8.1. Suspended wire cages in a commercial rabbitry.

The hutches or cages may be arranged in a number of different ways inside the building. The most common arrangement consists of rows of cages, with 2 rows opening onto a central walkway which makes servicing, feeding, and watering more practical. The walkway should be sufficiently wide for a feed or service cart and for servicing the cages. Cages should be firmly suspended from the frame structure so that there is no obstruction underneath them to interfere with routine cleaning. A more efficient use of space within the building, however, can be accomplished by means of multiple tiers of cages, that is, one or more rows of cages above the other. It should be obvious that with a multiple tier system, the problem of manure removal is more difficult. This may be accomplished by litter pans placed under each row of cages or by a sheet of metal sloping in such a way that wash water can be used to remove the manure and urine which should empty into a drain.

Ample storage for feed and other supplies should be provided in the building, and this area should be well enclosed to prevent the entry of rats and other pests.

Self-contained, outside hutches were formerly used extensively and are still used to some extent, primarily by the small-scale producers or others having a few animals. Self-contained hutches cannot be recommended except for these limited types of housing, and unless these units are particularly well designed, they normally cannot provide as good overall protection from the weather as can the larger buildings. Small housing units maintained outside of a building vary quite widely in size, shape, and design. The basic construction materials are normally wood and welded wire. Many are made with a wire floor and sides attached to a wooden frame. In some cases, the framework is constructed separately and the wire cage suspended under the roof. The cages must be constructed so that protection from the weather is maximum and yet ventilation is adequate. The roof should be made of a material that reflects, rather than absorbs, heat.

Research or laboratory rabbits and many of those produced for research are housed in buildings which are more expensive and elaborate. These are normally masonry buildings with sealed concrete floors or the equivalent, and most of them have mechanical control systems to provide the desirable environmental conditions. Multiple tier cages suspended on racks is the most common method of housing rabbits in the laboratory. Litter pans for collection of excreta or pans that can be flushed with water are required.

CAGES AND HUTCHES

CAGE SIZE

Cage size varies depending on the breed or breeds being maintained. Dimensions indicated in Table 8.1 are those most widely used in commercial rabbitries. Sizes are indicated for the three general size groups of rabbits, for a single rabbit, and for a doe and litter. The minimum amount of floor space currently required by federal regulations, exclusive of that occupied by feed and water containers, is indicated in Table 8.2. Cages must be large enough for rabbits to make normal postural adjustments and to provide adequate freedom of movement.

CAGE MATERIALS AND CONSTRUCTION

The material most widely used for rabbit cages is woven wire or hardware cloth which is galvanized after being welded. As long as the coating remains intact, the metal does not rust. Once this coating wears away or is damaged, corrosion is rapid. Stainless steel cages are used primarily in the laboratory. These are much more expensive, but are noncorrosive and last for long periods.

Two measurements are needed to identify wire used for rabbit cages. The grid or mesh refers to the size of openings between strands of wire. One-half inch (2 x 2 mesh) means that the openings are 1/2 inch or that there are 2 openings per linear inch. Wire is available in 1/2 inch x 1/2 inch, 1/2 inch x 1 inch, 5/8 inch x 1 inch, and other sizes. The other important measurement is the size or diameter of the strands of wire. This is referred to as the gauge, and the larger the gauge number the

TABLE 8.1. CAGE DIMENSIONS AND FLOOR MESH SIZE
FOR HOUSING COMMERCIAL RABBITS

Breed Size	Width in.	cm	Length in.	cm	Height in.	cm	Floor Mesh (in.)
Single rabbits							
Small	30	76	18–24	46–61	18	46	1/2 × 1/2
Medium	30	76	24–30	61–76	18	46	1/2 × 1 or 5/8 × 1
Large	30	76	30–36	76–91	18	46	5/8 × 1
Doe and litter							
Small	30	76	30–36	76–91	18	46	1/2 × 1/2
Medium	30	76	36–48	91–122	18	46	1/2 × 1 or 5/8 × 1
Large	30	76	48	122	18	46	5/8 × 1

smaller the wire. Particular attention should be given to the mesh and gauge of wire used for the floor. Grid openings must be large enough to allow fecal pellets to pass through readily yet small enough to provide comfort and prevent the feet from becoming entangled. Wire which is 1/2 x 1/2 inch is recommended for the small breeds, 1/2 x 1 inch or 5/8 x 1 inch for the medium-weight breeds, and 5/8 x 1 inch for the large breeds. Wire for the floor should be at least 15 gauge, and preferably 14 for the medium-weight breeds. If smaller wire (16 or 18 gauge) is used, the floor is likely to sag unless additional support is provided (Fig. 8.2).

The wire for sides and tops of cages may be of a larger gauge

TABLE 8.2. MINIMUM CAGE SPACE FOR RABBITS

Category	Individual Weights (lbs)	Minimum Space per Rabbit (sq in.)
Groups	3–5	144
	6–8	288
	9 or more	432
Individual adults	3–5	180
	6–8	360
	9–11	540
	12 or more	720
Nursing females	3–5	576
	6–8	720
	9–11	864
	12 or more	1080

SHEET METAL

Approximate Thickness and Number of Gauge	Thickness, Inches
11	.1196
12	.1046
14	.0747
16	.0598
18	.0478
20	.0359
22	.0299
24	.0239

WIRE

Approximate Size and Number of Gauge	Thickness, Inches
7	.1770
9	.1483
10	.1350
12	.1055
14	.0800
16	.0625
18	.0475

WOVEN WIRE CLOTH

No. 18 Ga. 3 Mesh   No. 16 Ga. 2 Mesh

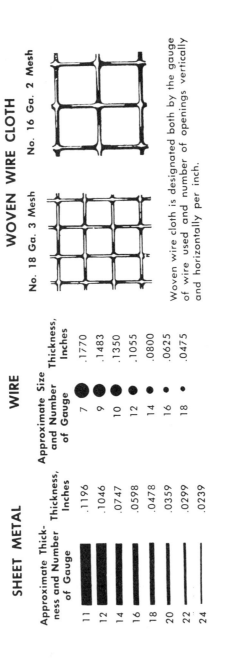

Woven wire cloth is designated both by the gauge of wire used and number of openings vertically and horizontally per inch.

Fig. 8.2. Identification of the gauge for sheet metal and wire and mesh size for woven wire. (Photo courtesy Hoeltge, Inc., Cincinnati, Oh., and Interstate Printers and Publishers, Danville, Ill.)

than that for the floor but should be of sufficient diameter to provide strength and rigidity. Size of mesh for the sides may also be different from that of the floor, but it should be sufficiently small to keep out rodents that might have entered the building.

Cages may be constructed with square or rectangular sides and tops or with rounded or curved tops (quonset type). They may be made in single units or in multiples of two, three, or more. Multiple units joined together are most economical in terms of construction, but long units are more difficult to handle if they are to be removed for cleaning or other purposes. Doors may be hinged at the top, side, or bottom. Doors of littering cages must be large enough to permit passage of the nest box. If doors are to swing into the cage, care must be taken to insure that they can open adequately with the nest box inside.

Wood is not a desirable material for cage construction. Rabbits gnaw wood and it absorbs water and urine, making good sanitation more difficult. If wood is used it should be limited to the framework, and the inner portion of the cage should be wire. Treated wood should be avoided if it is in contact with rabbits since treated materials may be injurious.

Cages may be purchased prefabricated or they may be easily constructed from wire available in most areas. Details of construction methods can vary and will not be presented, but a study of suitably constructed cages is helpful for the beginner if he plans to build his own.

LOCATION

Several factors must be considered in choosing the location for a rabbitry. A shaded area is desirable, particularly if a metal roof is to be used. The site should have well-drained soil, or some type of drainage should be provided for removal of rainwater as well as any wash water used for cleaning the facility.

The building or structure should also be placed away from populated areas. Even under the best of sanitary conditions, some odor from the rabbitry can be expected and this may be offensive to people. The facility should be in an area which is free of excessive noise, smoke, fumes, or other pollutants; it should be protected from predators, particularly from dogs. Important factors to be considered are city and county ordinances concerning the housing of animals. All such regulations must be observed. The location should be convenient for labor and easily accessible.

FEEDING EQUIPMENT

Many different kinds of feeders are used. Self-feeders which may contain several days supply of feed are desirable for does with litters. These may be attached to the cage so that feed can be added from the outside. Individual crocks, usually made of heavy porcelain, are also frequently used. Lightweight metal containers are easily overturned and undesirable unless attached to the cage. Feeding devices should be 3–4 inches high or raised to that height to minimize contamination of the feed by feces, urine, or water.

Hay racks, if used, should be attached to the upper portion of the cage. In duplex or multiple unit cages, the upper portion between units is often formed into a hay rack.

WATERING EQUIPMENT

An adequate supply of fresh, clean water is a requirement for good rabbit production. In small rabbitries (approximately 25 cages or less), water is normally provided in individual bowls or cups filled by hand. These containers should provide adequate amounts of water, not be readily overturned or contaminated with urine and feces, and be easily cleaned and sanitized. A common type of container is the heavy, glazed porcelain crock, although metal containers are used also. Waterers should be high enough (3–4 inches) to make water accessible, but not low enough for feet and dewlaps to become wet while the animal is drinking. Frequently the container is not large enough for a doe with a litter, and an insufficient amount of water can result in poor growth and low weaning weight. A female and a normal size litter of about 5 weeks old or older will drink a gallon or more of water per day.

In the laboratory and in certain other types of housing, water is supplied by means of inverted bottles fitted with sipper tubes. These are attached to the outside of the cage and the end of the tube is passed through the cage wall (Fig. 8.3). Advantages of this method are that cage space is not occupied by water containers, the water supply cannot be contaminated, and dewlaps cannot become wet. More time and labor, however, are required to fill and clean the equipment.

Fig. 8.3. Cages and rack for housing rabbits in a laboratory. (Photo courtesy Hoeltge, Inc., Cincinnati, Oh.)

Automatic watering devices deliver water to individual cages through a system of pipes and individual valves for each cage. The initial cost of these systems is such that they are usually limited to commercial production units of about twenty-five cages or more. Several different kinds of automatic waterers are manufactured by many different companies. One type, commonly called the "dewdrop" system, operates on a low water pressure utilizing a pressure-reducing valve or an overhead tank or reservoir. Although this system is the least expensive, it is not as satisfactory as the others; water may leak or the delivery ports may become clogged and fail to deliver water. Other systems operating on higher water pressure have valves which the animal must move or activate in order to obtain water. These systems are more expensive but are more satisfactory. Operational failures, however, can occur in any automatic watering system; it may leak or collect debris and fail to deliver water. Without careful and frequent checking it is impossible to know whether or not each rabbit is obtaining adequate water. Electric heat cables may be installed to protect these watering devices from freezing in cold climates.

NEST BOXES

At the time of littering, the doe will require a nest box in which to produce and hide her young. If some type of enclosure is not provided, she must deliver on the cage floor, and frequently several of the young will die from exposure or lack of care. Since this box must be placed in the cage, it is necessary that it be small enough to pass through the door and not occupy an excessive amount of the floor area, yet be large enough for the doe to easily enter and move about. A box 10–12 inches wide by 20 inches long and about 12 inches high is suitable for medium breeds. Smaller sizes can be used for Dutch rabbits and other small breeds.

Nest boxes may be constructed of wood or sheet metal (Fig. 8.4). Although wood is used, it is not as desirable as metal since it may be gnawed, and it is almost impossible to clean and sani-

Fig. 8.4. Examples of metal and wooden nest boxes.

tize properly. Exposed edges of the wood may be covered with sheet metal to prevent gnawing. Sheet metal boxes should be made with a masonite or wood floor for better insulation. Sheet metal or tempered masonite should not be used for the floor since it tends to cause spraddle hocks in the young. In very cold weather, the nest box should be fitted with a double floor containing hay, straw, or other bedding between the two layers. In very hot weather floors of wire or pegboard will provide better ventilation and cooling. A nest box made entirely of wire is also available and may be fitted with a disposable cardboard liner which makes it useful in cooler weather. Cages may be made with a nest box area as a permanent part of the cage. The cage floor is modified with a submerged area comparable to the nest box size, and nesting material is added at the time of kindling. Another method involves the attachment of a nest box under the cage in a way that permits it to be pulled out in the manner of a desk drawer. This provides convenient access for examining the litter with minimum disturbance to the doe, but construction is slightly more difficult and expensive.

MISCELLANEOUS EQUIPMENT

The following additional items of equipment and labor-saving devices are useful in a rabbitry. Number of items, cost, and type can vary depending upon the needs of the operation.

A service or utility cart can serve many purposes. It can be purchased or constructed from some simple, wheeled cart. It may have a combination of units: feed bin, examination and treatment platform, scales, and small holding pen. In the larger rabbitries, these units may be on separate carts. The examining table or platform should not have a slick surface, and a covering of carpet or burlap is often used.

An accurate scale is important for weighing rabbits and feed. The lightweight spring-type scales are least expensive, but are usually less accurate than balance-type scales. Any scale should be checked periodically for accuracy.

Restraining devices are useful for holding rabbits for tattooing, treatment of ear canker, other treatments, or for drawing blood samples from the ear. These may be purchased or constructed from wood (Fig. 8.5). The restraining box should be adjustable so that it can be used with different size rabbits.

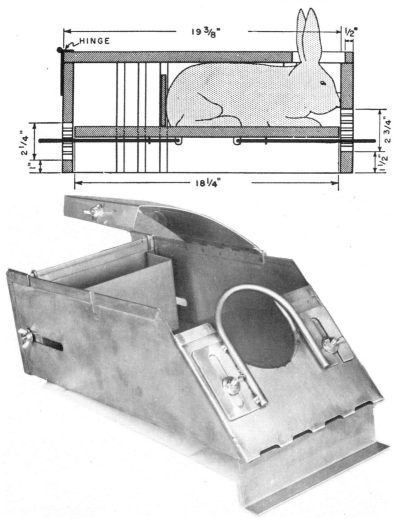

Fig. 8.5. Restraining devices. Upper, device which may be constructed of wood. Lower, metal restrainer. (Upper photo courtesy U.S. Department of Agriculture. Lower photo courtesy Hoeltge, Inc., Cincinnati, Oh.)

Transport or carrying cages are helpful for moving rabbits or for holding them temporarily. These are smaller than housing cages and may be constructed with handles for ease of carrying.

Adequate protected storage space for small items, including refrigerated storage for drugs and biological supplies, is also important.

REFERENCES

Arrington, L. R. 1970. Colony housing of domestic rabbits. Fla. Agr. Expt. Sta. Mimeo Report AN 70–7.

Guthrie, D. 1969. New concepts in rabbit housing. Small Stock Mag. 53 (No. 5): 7.

Johnson, H. D., C. S. Cheng, and A. C. Ragsdale. 1958. Environmental physiology and shelter engineering with special reference to domestic animals. 46. Comparison of the effects of environmental temperature on rabbits and cattle. Part 2. Influence of rising environmental temperature on the physiological reactions of rabbits and cattle. Mo. Agr. Expt. Sta. Res. Bul. 648.

Johnson, H. D., A. C. Ragsdale, and C. S. Cheng. 1957. Environmental physiology and shelter engineering with special reference to domestic animals. 45. Comparison of the effects of environmental temperature on rabbits and cattle. Part 1. Influence of construction and environmental temperature ($50°$–$80°$) on the growth responses and physiological reaction of rabbits and cattle. Mo. Agr. Expt. Sta. Res. Bul. 646.

United States Department of Agriculture. Economic Research Service. 1973. Hutches for rabbits. Misc. Pub. 1267. Washington, D.C.

9. MANAGEMENT

Management involves all of the plans and procedures necessary for the efficient, economical, and safe operation of a rabbitry; it concerns the individual animal as well as the whole colony. Management is closely related to feeding, breeding, and disease control, and thus many of the management factors concerning these phases of rabbit production have been included in those respective chapters. There are, however, certain important procedures and operations not previously discussed: handling, identification, registration, culling and selection, record keeping, breeding plans and schedules, feeding schedules, and methods of sanitation and disease control are important aspects of management. The building design and construction as well as the arrangement or rearrangement of equipment for most efficient operation are also matters of management. Proper management can often mean the difference between success and failure or can affect the degree of success. The nature of management is such that no specific rules or lists of procedures can be given, for it involves plans and decision making often related to a specific type of operation. Elaborate facilities and equipment, highly paid labor, and good quality initial animals will not substitute for the necessary management decisions required for successful operation. Good management can result from good planning and preparation, experience, knowledge of all phases of rabbit production, and careful analysis of factors relating to management procedures.

177

HANDLING RABBITS

The production of rabbits for any purpose requires that they be handled when transferred to other cages, for examination, restraint in treatment, tattooing, judging in shows, etc. Using proper methods, rabbits may be easily handled without injury to the animal or to the handler. The method chosen should be used consistently so that the animal becomes accustomed to being handled. Rabbits seldom bite, but they can scratch if not lifted and held properly. When approaching a rabbit to be handled, one should proceed slowly and carefully so that it is not frightened. Rabbits are lifted by grasping the skin over the shoulders; they must never be lifted by the ears, but the ears should be included or held along with the skin over the shoulders. When holding the rabbit for a period of time, one hand should be placed below the hindquarters for additional support. The animal is less likely to struggle and scratch if held next to the person's body (Fig. 9.1). Young rabbits may be lifted and held by grasping with the hand over the lower loin area just forward of the rear legs. Holding or handling by the skin over the shoulder is preferred, but the latter may be used with young animals. When it is necessary to restrain for tattooing, treatment of ear canker, or drawing a blood sample from the ear, a restraining box may be used. Some types of treatment and examination may be administered without the use of a box, provided the rabbit is adequately held, although an additional person may be required to hold the animal. When handling a rabbit for any purpose, effort should be made to prevent struggling which can occasionally result in a back injury to the animal.

IDENTIFICATION

Identification of each rabbit in a colony is important since records are not possible without a good system of animal identification. The preferred and most common method is the tattoo on the inner surface of the left ear. This surface is relatively free of hair, and the tattoo properly applied is permanent and can be

Fig. 9.1. Method of holding rabbit. Upper, adult rabbit. Lower, young rabbit. (Photo courtesy Ann Randles, Ocala, Fl.)

read easily. Tattooing involves the impregnation of a permanent ink or dye into the skin. Several types of tattooing devices can be purchased: a hand needle or vibrating needle may be used to scratch the surface of the ear into which the dye is then rubbed; clamp sets made of dyes with letters or numbers which easily penetrate and imprint the dye into the skin are also available.

There is no required system of numbers to be used, although numbers selected should not be arbitrary but should represent useful information about the animal. Those selected can represent blood line, source, or other information desired by the breeder. Colony or herd numbers are placed in the left ear. The right ear is reserved for the registration number if the animal is to be registered.

Another method of identifying rabbits is with a band on one of the rear legs. Leg bands are normally used only on small breeds, such as the Netherland Dwarf, because of the small ear size. Ear clips and notching have been used in the past, but are not recommended since ear clips are frequently torn out, and both methods are harmful to ear tissue.

RECORD KEEPING

Numerous records are required in a well-managed rabbitry. The time spent in maintaining good records is well invested and adequate amounts should be allotted for this task. A common mistake is the failure to record data before it is forgotten. For this reason, a place for the easy recording of information is very important. The hutch card attached to each cage is useful for this purpose, but it must be considered a temporary record since it may become soiled, torn, or lost. Information on the hutch card should be transferred regularly to a permanent record maintained in the office.

Records can be very extensive and elaborate or they can be minimal, depending upon the nature and purpose of the enterprise; they should include animal data as well as business or financial information as indicated in chapter 10. With good animal records, it is possible to identify the good producers and cull those which are less desirable. In selecting breeding stock, it is always well to choose from those which have been good producers, and it is possible to identify these animals only if adequate records are available. It should also be emphasized that complete ancestral records are required for the registration of rabbits. The more important records which should be maintained for each animal are: identification number, pedigree, sex, date born, breeding date, litter date, weight at weaning, and number in litter.

Methods of record keeping need not follow any specific procedure, but it is important that pertinent information be recorded in a systematic way. A producer may wish to design his own record system. Several types of forms and materials are available, and most feed companies will provide hutch cards and record sheets for the necessary data. There are forms for doe and buck records and monthly production summary charts. Modification of the more typical forms may be made. Figure 9.2 illustrates a record form, printed on 5 x 7 cards, which can be used for either the doe or the buck. The reverse side of each card contains space arranged to record the rabbit's pedigree. A separate card can be made for summarizing mortality or other summary records. Cards may be color coded as an easy means of identifying breeds, varieties, strains, or other classifications. They may be subfiled according to litter, weaning time, buck, doe, prospective breeder, or other categories. Many other adaptations of a card record system may be made, and the ease of filing and sorting makes a card record system practical and useful.

REGISTRATION

Purebred rabbits may be registered if adequate records are maintained to establish individual ancestry. The American Rabbit Breeders Association (ARBA) is the official organization for this registration. Any purebred rabbit 6 months of age for which the parents, grandparents, and great-grandparents are known is eligible for registration even though none of its ancestors was registered. A rabbit eligible for registration must be examined by a

NO. _____

BORN _____   SEX _____   BREED _____

DATE	BREEDING	LITTERED	NO. BORN	NO. RAISED	

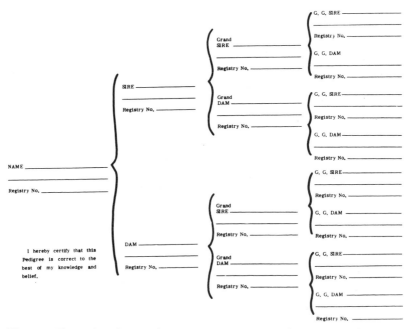

Fig. 9.2. Example of record cards. Upper, production record. Lower, pedigree on reverse of card.

licensed registrar for markings, coat and eye color, type, and weight. If the rabbit has no disqualifications as defined by the breed standard, it can then be registered.

On registering a rabbit, a number corresponding to the one on the registration form is tattooed into its right ear. The form is then sent to the ARBA by the registrar for recording, and the owner receives a registration certificate for each animal. The form will have a colored seal denoting the registration of the rabbit's ancestors; a red seal indicates that only the parents are registered; a red and white seal that the parents and grandparents are registered, and a red, white, and blue seal that the three previous generations of parents are registered.

A small fee, set by the ARBA, is charged for each registration. Because there is a fee involved, the desirability of having an entire colony registered must be evaluated. Those breeders raising and expecting to sell primarily breeding stock should have their animals registered. The buyer purchasing such stock prefers those with the red, white, and blue registration, for this demonstrates that the rabbits' ancestors have met the breed standards for at least three generations. Rabbits with this registration are usually sold for a higher price than those with other types or with no registration. The fancy breeder and semicommercial breeder should maintain registered stock; however, it is impractical for the large commercial producers to do so.

Registrars are licensed by the ARBA. To obtain a license, the applicant must be a member of the association for three years and must work five rabbit shows prior to taking the registrars' examination. The requirement of working with a judge at five shows is to familiarize the individual with a number of different breeds of rabbits and their breed standards. After completing the required number of shows and being approved by the judges under whom he has worked, the individual may then take the examination. If he passes, he becomes a licensed registrar and is eligible to register any purebred rabbit under the auspices of the ARBA.

BREEDING SCHEDULES

Breeding programs relating to genetics and animal improvement were outlined in chapter 5. Practical application and scheduling of these programs are matters of management. The program used and its management will depend upon purpose and type of the rabbit enterprise, its size, and other factors. The only fixed parameter in a breeding schedule is the 31–32-day gestation period. Others such as breeding age, weaning age, number of litters per year, and time of breeding can be controlled by the breeder.

A typical breeding schedule for medium breeds (New Zealand, Californian) involves mating the does when they are about 6 months old. The young are weaned at 8 weeks and the doe is re-bred within 2–3 days. This schedule results in 4 litters per year per doe provided there are no failures in breeding. A more intensive schedule followed by many producers involves re-breeding the doe at 6 weeks. The young may be weaned at 6 weeks or they may remain with the doe for another 2 weeks. This schedule can result in 5 litters per year. The newest concept in breeding schedules consists of weaning the young at 4 weeks, utilizing special creep feeds for them, and immediately re-breeding the doe. Such a schedule can result in 6 litters per year; however, increased costs are involved since more cage space is required and creep feeds are more expensive than regular feeds. Production of 5 litters per year per doe improves production rate over the traditional schedule of 4 litters per year and does not appear to alter the doe replacement rate. With 6 or more litters per year, the replacement rate of breeding does frequently increases and mortality of the does and young is greater.

Breeders of fancy rabbits frequently maintain does that function only to produce litters. The desirable young at birth are fostered with another lactating doe and the doe is re-bred. With this schedule, a doe can produce 10 litters per year. The purpose is to produce as many quality offspring from a given doe as is possible during her breeding life.

Once a schedule has been selected, only good management can put it into effect and insure that breeding and weaning occur as planned.

SELECTION AND CULLING

Selection of breeding stock, whether it is purchased or chosen from offspring within the herd, can play a major role in the important task of improving animals. This should involve the study of production records, careful physical examination of the animal, and application of the principles of inheritance (chapters 2 and 5). The breeding of animals which are carelessly and randomly selected can result in deterioration of quality in a short time. Goals should be to keep production rate high (8–10 per litter), obtain good meat quality and high dressing percentage, and improve breed characteristics. A specific improvement of offspring over parents within a breed may require four to five generations.

Culling and selection of young rabbits for future breeders begins at 8 weeks when they are ready for market. Selection at this time is based primarily on weight. Any young of medium-weight breeds that do not weigh 4 pounds at 8 weeks should be culled. Of those that are large enough, further selection should be made on the basis of type, smoothness of hips, width of loin and shoulders, and other desirable traits. As the selected rabbits mature, there should be a further evaluation of the animals. Any rabbit that did not develop as expected or has an apparent undesirable characteristic which would be transmitted to the offspring should be culled. Those which have thin foot pads and thus may be predisposed to sore hocks should be culled. Selected breeders should be free of respiratory infections and other health problems. They should be chosen from litters of 7 or more young since offspring from small litters tend to produce small litters.

SANITATION AND CLEANING

Management of sanitation practices and procedures is a major factor in disease control. The objective is to prevent or minimize the spread of disease, and a carefully followed program is essential for maintenance of effective sanitation. Plans and procedures should be considered in relation to the methods by which diseases are spread. Considerable labor and some expense are required and there are few short cuts. Procedures for cleaning and disinfecting are varied, and a specific method applicable to each situation is not possible. Common sense, hard labor, and a few basic principles are important.

The program should begin with the design, construction, and arrangement of the building and rabbit cages in a way that tends to reduce the spread of microorganisms and makes routine cleaning easier. Buildings should provide necessary protection and be well ventilated, dry, and adequately lighted. Crowding rabbits into a poorly ventilated, moist area is asking for trouble. Floors of sealed concrete or other hard, nonporous materials are most easily cleaned and are preferred. Cages should have adequate ventilation and wire floors.

Manure should be removed regularly and not be allowed to accumulate. Daily removal is desirable, but a weekly or longer schedule is satisfactory in some situations. A thorough cleaning, less frequently, can be better than a careless daily cleaning.

Cages, feed and watering equipment, and other items coming in contact with rabbits should be cleaned and sanitized on a regular schedule rather than waiting until they are visibly soiled. There is no specific rule for frequency of cleaning, and, although daily cleaning would be ideal, it is generally impractical. For the average rabbitry, weekly cleaning and sanitizing of these items should be sufficient. It is important that cages, equipment, and premises be cleaned and sanitized more frequently when there is a disease problem. However, under no circumstances should cleaning be postponed until a disease appears.

In cleaning equipment, all adhering manure or soil should be scraped away, followed by a plain water rinse to remove additional debris. Items should then be washed in hot water containing a suitable cleaning compound. A strong bristle brush should be used, but wire brushes should be avoided as they damage the galvanized coating on cages and other items constructed of galvanized metal. After washing, the items should be rinsed to remove the cleaning solution and disinfected to kill any remaining organisms. If the wash water could be maintained at 180°F the heat would be adequate to sanitize the equipment satisfactorily; however, it is difficult to maintain water at this temperature for washing except in a mechanical cage-washing machine. Equipment cleaned in water not heated to that temperature should be treated, after rinsing, with a chemical sanitizing agent. There are numerous types of sanitizing agents; chlorine solution is a good example. These are added to plain water, and the clean items are dipped or the solution is sprayed on. Several precautions should be observed when using such agents. They should be applied in the recommended strength or concentration. If the solution is too weak, the proper degree of sanitation will not be achieved; if it is too strong, some compounds, particularly chlorine, may corrode the metal. Items must be thoroughly cleaned before disinfecting since the disinfectant does not penetrate pockets of remaining soil which can harbor microorganisms. In addition, organic matter such as manure or other debris on improperly cleaned equipment tends to weaken the disinfectant solution. After sanitizing, the equipment should be rinsed with clean water to remove residual chemicals.

The suitable cleaning of rabbit cages can be a problem and a real chore because of their size and because many are permanently attached to the building framework. It may be necessary to wash the cages in place and spray the disinfectant on after rinsing. Any excess moisture in the rabbit house is undesirable, and washing the cages in place tends to add to the moisture problem unless the building floor is adequately drained.

A heating torch or blow torch is sometimes used to disinfect cages which are permanently attached. The heat will disinfect those areas adequately reached by the torch. With sufficient application it will also burn away adhering hair and manure, but excessive heat is damaging to the wire and causes discoloration. A torch, therefore, is recommended only when other methods are not available.

In research laboratories and in large rabbitries, automatic cage washers are generally used. These provide the hot washing solutions under pressure for cleaning, followed by a rinse cycle. Temperature of the washing solution can be maintained at

180°F, sufficient to kill pathogenic organisms. These washers are rather expensive and generally not practical for the average producer. Other cleaning aids and devices are available and money invested in these is well spent. An adequate supply of hot water is essential and a cleaning room separate from the rabbit quarters is desirable. Sinks or vats of appropriate size for washing, rinsing, and disinfecting are needed. A hand pressure sprayer is useful for applying a disinfectant to cages and equipment which cannot be dipped.

SHIPMENT

Rabbits may be shipped long distances and may be transported by air to any country. Shipment places stress on the animals and only healthy ones should be moved. Appropriate containers should be used and special care and handling exercised in all phases of transport. Containers should be clearly labeled to show that they contain live animals when carried by common carrier.

Shipping containers must be made of inexpensive materials for they are considered disposable. Crates of thin wood supported or bound with wire are often used for rabbits. These must provide adequate ventilation, some seclusion to help prevent fright, protection from changes in weather, and they must be large enough to allow each rabbit sufficient space to turn about freely and to make normal postural adjustments. The label, in addition to noting the presence of live animals, should also carry any special instructions for care. Any feeding or watering instructions or other special needs must be arranged for with the carrier beforehand. During shipment, animals should not be exposed to excessive heat or cold or to other adverse weather conditions. The present regulations also state that no more than fifteen rabbits may be transported in the same primary enclosure.

If shipment requires more than 6 hours, rabbits must be supplied with water and feed. This may be the regular feed and water or a suitable quantity and quality of vegetables for the period of transit. Rabbits not accustomed to eating fresh vegetables may refuse them, and if this method is used, the animals should be preconditioned to consumption of greens or root crops. Prior to shipment, current airline or carrier regulations as well as federal regulations regarding transport of animals should be determined. A health certificate from a veterinarian may be required.

REFERENCES

Bel, L., M. Prud'hon, and A. Benhacing. 1971. Early weaning of young rabbits and continued production in does. (Text in Spanish.) Advances Aliment. Mejora Anim. 10: 973–81.

Broadfoot, J. 1969. Hand rearing rabbits. J. Inst. Anim. Tech. 20: 91–99.

Hagen, K. W. 1974. Colony husbandry. In *The Biology of the Laboratory Rabbit*, eds. S. H. Weisbroth, R. E. Flatt, and A. L. Kraus. Academic Press: New York.

Hills, D. M., and I. McDonald. 1956. Hand raising of rabbits. Nature (London) 178: 704–5.

Kaplan, H. M. 1958. Tattoo patterns for rabbits. Proc. Anim. Care Panel 8: 20.

Prud'hon, M., and L. Bel. 1968. Early weaning of young rabbits and reproduction in does. Ann. Zootech. 17: 23–30.

10. ECONOMICS, MARKETING, PROCESSSING, BY-PRODUCTS

Economic factors are important in the planning and operation of any rabbitry, including those in which rabbits are raised for pets or as a hobby. The financial success of a commercial operation depends upon many economic as well as production factors. Once a rabbit enterprise is in operation, it should be continuously evaluated to determine where costs may be reduced and profits increased. This analysis should utilize basic economic principles and information relating to various aspects of rabbit production.

Unfortunately, extensive and reliable economic data relating to the rabbit industry and production are not available. The economic research necessary to provide the information needed for thorough analysis has not been performed. Limited information, however, is available, and with the application of economic principles, some basic guidelines can be established.

SIZE OF RABBITRY

The size of a rabbit production unit is usually defined by the number of producing or breeding does. In order to maintain a specific number of such does, the breeder should have the proper number of herd bucks and replacement animals available. One mature breeding buck is required for each 10–15 breeding females. In addition, growing does and bucks must be available to replace those removed after effective reproductive life has passed, those which die, and those culled as poor producers. The average reproductive life of the rabbit is about 3 years, so for each 100 females at least 35 must be replaced each year.

The number of rabbits to be maintained in a unit is governed by the space available for housing, amount of labor available, market outlets, personal preference, and possibly other factors. Space requirements have been discussed in chapter 8. It is important that the number of rabbits does not exceed available labor. Occasionally, a producer will make the mistake of beginning with too many rabbits or allowing the unit to grow beyond the limits of labor to care for it properly. About 5–8 man hours per year per breeding doe are required for adequate care. A husband and wife team devoting essentially full time to rabbit production should be able to maintain a unit consisting of about 300 or more breeding does.

The nature of rabbit production is such that both large and small units can be satisfactory and profitable. In large commercial rabbitries, the construction and arrangement of buildings, use of automated equipment, efficient use of labor, and purchase of feed in quantity result in less cost per doe unit than in small operations. In small rabbitries, most, if not all, labor is performed by family members, and this can contribute to success even though costs per doe unit may be higher.

No ideal rabbitry size can be recommended except on the basis of space, labor, and markets. An inexperienced, beginning producer should start with 10–15 breeding does and expand the colony as experience and markets permit. The experienced raiser may begin or maintain any number that may be effectively managed and profitably marketed.

CAPITAL OUTLAY

The initial capital outlay for beginning a production unit depends primarily upon cost of land, if it must be purchased, size and type of housing, and number of breeding animals to be purchased. No cost estimates can be provided here because of the great variation in land values and in construction, material, and labor costs in different regions. Individuals contemplating investment should visit existing operations in the locality and consult state land grant university personnel for information and assistance. Essential items required in the initial investment are: land, rabbit house or shed, cages or hutches, breeding stock, feeding and watering equipment, nest boxes, truck or other vehicle, scale, medications, and miscellaneous small tools and supplies.

The costs of land and buildings represent the two largest single items of initial investment, but the actual outlay will depend upon size of the operation. Often the rabbitry is operated on land already owned or otherwise available, and although this may not enter into the initial cost, it nevertheless represents an investment which is part of the total rabbitry. Types of buildings and space requirements have been indicated in chapter 8.

Costs of cages can vary greatly depending upon materials and whether they are purchased prefabricated or made by the producer. Materials can be purchased and cages may be constructed at less cost than prefabricated units.

Procedures and recommendations for purchase of breeding stock are indicated in chapter 2. The cost of a good breeding animal may be four to six times that of the average animal, but funds spent for quality breeding stock are well invested.

OPERATING EXPENSE

The major items of operating expense are labor and feed costs. The amount of labor required for the care and management of rabbits is greater per animal unit than for poultry and other animals of similar size. A major reason for this is the type of housing which requires an individual cage per rabbit. Each animal must be fed and each cage serviced separately. This difference in labor cost is readily apparent when rabbits are compared to poultry; large numbers of birds are housed together and can be fed and handled as a group. In addition, few of the chores required for raising rabbits have been automated and most are carried out by hand; automatic watering devices represent about the only automated procedure for rabbit production. Commercial rabbit production units requiring hired labor must calculate labor costs on the basis of employment rates in effect at the time. Assuming 8 hours of labor per doe per year, a 40-hour work week, and 50 weeks of actual work, one person should be able to care for a unit of 200 breeding does.

In most rabbitries labor is provided by family members and is not considered in the same way as it would be if an outside labor force had to be employed. In small units work schedules usually may be arranged so that the procedures can be carried out before or after other working hours if necessary. Labor is an important item, however, regardless of whether it is family or employed labor.

The other major operating cost is feed. Even if a certain portion of the feed is home grown, there are labor and other costs involved in its production and harvesting. Most feed, however, is commercially mixed and purchased from a dealer. Large production units or cooperatives may purchase feed in quantity at a reduced cost. Feeds vary in price and the cheapest is not always the most economical. If a low-cost feed does not promote the desirable growth and performance of the rabbits, it can be the most expensive. On the other hand, the most expensive is not always necessary. Information on nutrient composition may be obtained from the dealer or manufacturer and a quality-cost comparison made. In considering feed costs, reference should be made to chapter 6.

Many other miscellaneous expenses must also be added to the cost of operation: medications, electric and water supplies, cage and building repair, and replacement of equipment. Interest on investment should also be included as an expense item.

ECONOMIC AND FINANCIAL RECORDS

Adequate records are essential for determining profit or loss in a rabbit production unit. Guesses and estimates are insufficient. Records need not be elaborate, but they should be maintained systematically and should include all costs of production and income received. The manner in which these records are kept can vary, but it is important that they are maintained in a way that can be clearly understood at a later date. When rabbits are produced for one major purpose, such as for meat, it is often easy to overlook secondary or miscellaneous sales, such as the sale of a few breeders, the sale of a few as pets, or the slaughter of some animals for personal use. All of these represent a type of sale and therefore should be listed as income. For any one year or period of time for which calculations are made, the increased value of the herd (if numbers of animals have increased) must be included as an asset or as an investment. This would not represent an income for any one year or period, but it would be a long-term gain and therefore represent income.

A record of all expense items is also necessary. For tax records and other purposes, depreciation on building and equipment represents a type of expense. The proper accounting for labor of the family members is very difficult, but should be included. Such accounting is not required except when it is desirable to determine profit above all costs. In this case, a value must be assigned to family or unpaid labor devoted to the enterprise. When labor is employed, labor cost records should be maintained. Record books and forms for animal enterprises are available from county extension offices or the state extension service.

MARKETING

Marketing is one of the most important decision areas the producer faces. Improving production practices and internal economic efficiency benefits the operation, but the largest payoff for production improvement is usually through the market.

The channels and procedures by which rabbits are marketed have not been as well established and are not as uniform as those for the marketing of poultry and other types of livestock. There are different types of markets for rabbits and sometimes they must be located or cultivated. The new producer starting production where markets may not already exist should thoroughly investigate the market potential before he invests time and money. A frequent mistake of beginning producers is to start the operation, then find themselves with marketable animals before they have developed adequate outlets for sales. It is desirable in some cases to produce rabbits for more than one type of market. For example, if the major objective is to produce rabbits for sale as meat, it may be possible to sell the same type of rabbits for research or as breeders.

LABORATORY

Substantial markets for rabbits as laboratory animals exist and constitute the second largest income from commercial production; about 600,000 are used annually in this country. The breed in greatest demand for research is the New Zealand White, and more than 50 per cent of the rabbits used in laboratories are of this breed. The Dutch is next most widely used, but accounts for only about 2 per cent of the total. Prices paid for laboratory rabbits are usually higher than those paid for meat rabbits. However, these prices vary greatly, depending upon the strain of rabbit, its age, location, and other factors. The market for research rabbits is a rather specialized one and it must be viewed differently from that for meat rabbits. In general, research rabbits must be highly uniform, the conditions under which they were raised may need to be known by the user, and large numbers of a specific breed, strain, age, or sex may be required at one time; in some cases, a specific inbred strain may be required. The demands for research rabbits are likely to be sporadic and variable. Large numbers may be required by a laboratory at one time, followed by long periods when only a few, or none, are ordered. The only method of reducing this fluctuation is to have several research markets or a combination research and meat market.

Most, but not all, laboratory rabbits are supplied by producers or animal farms specializing in production of animals for research. Those breeders maintaining high quality animals suitable for research may market some of the animals for meat as well. The commercial producers of laboratory animals usually issue catalogs or price lists showing breeds or strains of animals, costs, and other information. Most users of laboratory animals will place orders as needed for research animals; some, however, will contract with a producer for an annual supply.

Federal regulations regarding the housing, care, and shipment of research animals must be observed. Current regulations should be determined from the U.S. Department of Agriculture.

MEAT

Since most rabbits produced are sold for meat, more attention has been given to marketing for this purpose than for the other uses. The meat market is based primarily on the sale of fryer rabbits, when they are about 8 weeks of age. Older rabbits are sold as roasters and stewers. The New Zealand and Californian breeds are most widely used for meat in this country. At 8 weeks of age, weaning rabbits of these breeds will produce carcasses weighing about 2 pounds, the size to which the retail market has become accustomed. This is not to indicate, however, that other breeds of rabbits cannot be sold for meat.

Most fryer rabbit producers sell their animals to a slaughter-processing plant or do their own slaughtering. Dressed rabbits are then sold to supermarkets and retail outlets and to hotels, restaurants, and institutions (the HRI trade). Rabbit meat must normally be marketed in urban areas, since the average American eats less than a quarter of a pound of rabbit per year. Thus, to assure the producer of a relatively stable market, consumers in larger cities must be reached.

An essential feature in the marketing of rabbits for meat is the availability of a processing or a slaughtering plant. The processor usually picks up rabbits from nearby producers on a regular basis, or the producer may deliver his own rabbits to the slaughtering plant. The producer and the processor agree on the price to be paid and the number of rabbits that can be handled per week or per month.

Prices for fryer rabbits generally do not vary greatly during a year. The most important factors affecting prices an individual producer receives are number and quality of animals delivered. The producer who can market large uniform lots of quality animals consistently through the year should expect to receive a higher price per head or per pound than one whose rabbits show great variation in weight, condition, and lot size. Retail stores and the HRI trade must have dependable volume and quality, and usually will not deal with individuals who cannot meet these requirements.

Relatively stable prices at levels that provide a fair return to the producer remove some market uncertainty. Price, however, is only one of the factors or *terms of sale* the producer must negotiate with the buyer.

Most rabbits are sold on a price per pound of live weight. It is important to determine, in the terms of sale, the time and place at which rabbits are to be weighed. If the animals are shipped for long distances or if they are held for a period of time without feed and water, live weight will be reduced. Agreement should also be reached regarding carcasses which may have to be condemned because of disease or some other abnormality. Although most rabbits are sold on a live weight basis, large volume facilities may market on the basis of carcass quality and yield. The time and method of payment also should be established in the terms of sale.

Cooperative marketing may offer distinct advantages in selling rabbits. Cooperatives can be formed by producers in a particular locality to provide facilities and/or services for mutual benefits. Any or all of the following might be provided: ownership and operation of a processing plant, purchase of feed and other supplies at advantageous prices or terms, transportation, or other marketing services. Normally producer-members provide funds for initial capital outlay and operating expense, but there may be different arrangements for a cooperative. A large cooperative may employ a manager, but major business decisions are made by a board of directors elected by producer members.

Many problems in the rabbit industry have been related to inconsistency of markets and the failure or inability of independent processors to remain in business. Marketing cooperatively could help to overcome these problems; and although they offer distinct advantages, relatively few rabbit cooperatives have been established. As the name implies, the operation is dependent upon cooperation among members. Certain rules and regulations must be agreed upon in establishment and operation of a cooperative, but there remains some independence for each producer. Those who work harder and can produce the animals more efficiently will certainly be rewarded in terms of income for their extra effort.

Marketing specialists in the various state agricultural universities or in other government agencies can frequently provide information and guidelines for establishment and operation of marketing cooperatives.

THE PROCESSING PLANT

Rabbits to be sold commercially for meat must be slaughtered in facilities approved by local, state, or federal agencies as applicable. Prior to the construction of a processing plant, the building requirements should be determined. The slaughtering facility should be constructed to handle the number of rabbits expected and should provide means for expansion if needed later. Elaborate structures and equipment are not required, but they should be easy to clean and meet sanitary regulations.

Figure 10.1 illustrates a basic floor plan which could be used for a small processing plant. Work areas in the facilities should include:

Holding room or area for pre-slaughter animals
Kill or slaughter floor
Room or separate area for dressing carcasses, packaging, cutting, etc.
Cold storage and freezing facilities
Showers and toilets
Office.

The holding room or area should be separate from the kill floor. It should provide adequate protection for animals awaiting slaughter and, if rabbits are to be held overnight, provisions for feed and water should be made. Floors in the work area should be tile or dense, minimum-skid concrete with adequate slope and drains to remove wash water. Walls should be of some waterproof material, and the structure should be well-lighted and ventilated. There must be adequate hot water and provision for

cleaning and sanitizing all equipment. Conveyers and other automated and mechanical equipment may be included. Work areas
should be convenient for personnel and provide as much labor-
saving equipment as is practical.

SLAUGHTERING AND DRESSING

Rabbits may be killed by one of two ways. The preferred method
is dislocation of the neck (Fig. 10.2). The rabbit is held firmly
by the rear legs and the head; it is stretched full length, then

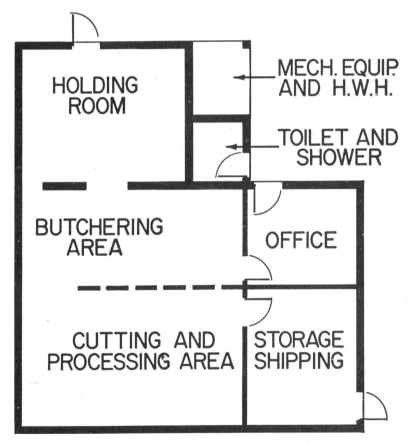

Fig. 10.1. Example of floor plan for small processing plant.

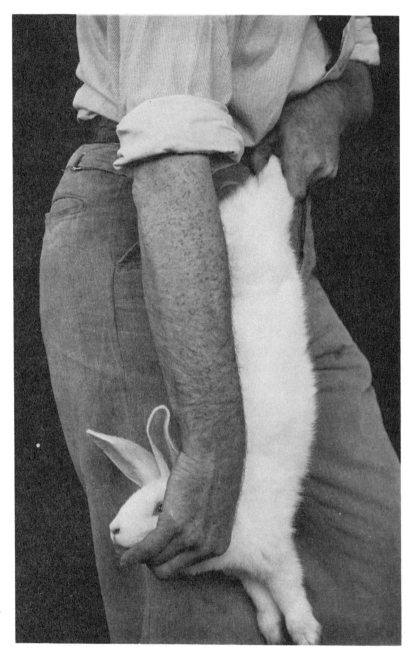

Fig. 10.2. Method of killing rabbit by dislocation of the neck. (Photo courtesy U.S. Department of Agriculture.)

with a hard, sharp pull, the head is bent backward to dislocate the neck. Or, the rabbit may be struck with a blunt stick or with the side of the hand, making a hard, quick blow to the skull just behind the ears. Both methods cause quick unconsciousness.

After dislocation or stunning, the rabbit is hung by one of the hind legs above the hock joint (Fig. 10.3). The head is immediately removed to allow complete bleeding. The forefeet are then removed. The next step is to cut the skin around the hock joints of the legs and then to cut between these points across the lower part of the body. The tail is cut away and the skin is then free to be pulled down and forward over the body. The skins of young or fryer age rabbits are easily removed in this way; it is more difficult to remove the skins of older rabbits. If skins are to be saved for marketing, they should be handled as indicated below (see Rabbit Skins and Pelts).

After the head, forefeet, and skin are removed, the carcass, while still hanging, is opened to remove the viscera. A cut is made on the lower part of the abdomen near the anus and a straight cut is made to the chest cavity. The intestinal tract and lungs are normally removed. Liver, kidneys, and heart remain with the carcass. The carcass is then removed from the hanger and the rear feet removed at the hock joint. The carcass should be washed with clean, cold water to remove hair and any other soil or debris, and should then be stored at a cold temperature, preferably at 35°F and not over 40°F. Dressed carcasses should not be held for any length of time in water as they absorb moisture, and absorbed water inside meat is considered a contaminant. When large numbers of rabbits are to be slaughtered, the operation on an assembly line basis is much more rapid and efficient.

Dressed rabbits may be sold whole or they may be cut into units such as those illustrated in Figure 10.4. Various types of marketing devices such as plastic cartons and trays are available for packaging one or more carcasses.

Fig. 10.3. Rabbit carcasses in various stages of skinning and removal of internal organs in processing for meat. (Photo courtesy U.S. Department of Agriculture.)

DRESSING PERCENTAGE

Dressing percentage is the relationship of the weight of a dressed carcass to the weight of the live animal expressed as a per cent. This will vary depending upon the quality of the animal at slaughter, breed, age, and amount of fat and the number of internal organs left with the carcass. Animals with good meat characteristics will have a higher dressing percentage than thin animals. Normally the liver, heart, and kidneys remain with the carcass and are included in the carcass weight.

Animals which are in average condition or slightly better than average should have a dressing percentage of 55 per cent, and good quality animals reach a dressing percentage of 60 per cent

TABLE 10.1. DRESSING PERCENTAGE OF NEW ZEALAND
AND DUTCH RABBITS AT DIFFERENT AGES

	New Zealand	Dutch
8 weeks	55.9	60.3
13 weeks	59.2	63.3
Mature	58.2	62.8

or higher. The data in Table 10.1 were obtained with New Zealand and Dutch rabbits of different ages which had been fed a commercial rabbit feed. Carcass weights included heart, liver, and kidneys. The dressing percentages of the Dutch were greater than those of the New Zealand. The percentage also increased from 8 to 13 weeks of age, but declined slightly in the mature rabbits. Mature rabbits in this study had been limit-fed, and this may account in part for the lower dressing percentage. Normally, dressing percentage increases with age until the rabbit approaches maturity.

RABBIT MEAT

Nutrient composition of rabbit meat and that for other common food animals is listed in Table 10.2. Rabbit meat is high in protein, fairly low in fat, and compares favorably with other meats in terms of the other nutrients supplied.

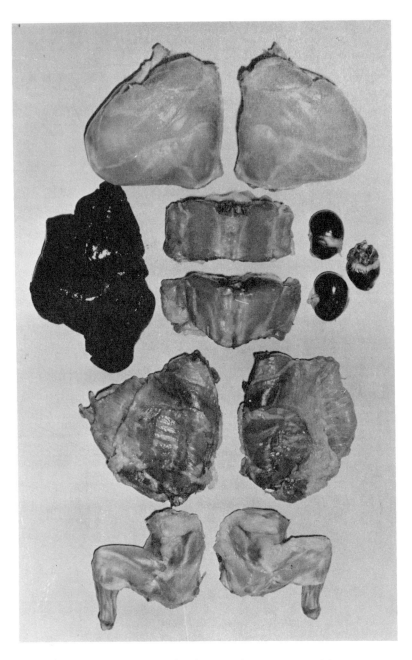

Fig. 10.4. Standard cuts of meat from rabbit carcasses. (Photo courtesy U.S. Department of Agriculture.)

TABLE 10.2. Composition of Rabbit and Other Meats
(per 100 grams)

	Water (%)	Energy (kcal)	Protein (%)	Fat (%)	Ca (mg)	P (mg)	Fe (mg)	Thiamine (mg)	Ribo-flavin (mg)	Niacin (mg)
Rabbit, domesticated, flesh only	70.0	162	21.0	8.0	20	352	1.3	.08	.06	12.8
Chicken, fryers, flesh, skin, and giblets	75.7	124	18.6	4.9	12	201	1.9	.07	.38	5.6
Beef, carcass, choice grade, total edible, trimmed	56.7	301	17.4	25.1	10	161	2.6	.07	.15	4.2
Lamb, trimmed cuts, choice grade	61.0	263	16.5	21.3	10	147	1.2	.15	.20	4.8
Pork, fresh, carcass, medium fat, trimmed lean cuts	56.3	308	15.7	26.7	9	175	2.3	.76	.18	4.1

SOURCE: Composition of Foods, Agriculture Handbook 8, Agricultural Research Service, USDA, 1963.

The flesh of rabbits is all white and pleasant tasting, and that from fryer-age rabbits is very tender. As is the case with other animals, however, the meat from old rabbits is less tender. Traditionally, rabbit meat has been prepared for the table in much the same way as poultry and it lends itself to a variety of cooking methods.

Rabbit meat may be frozen for storage or shipment using procedures similar to those used for poultry or other meats. Freezing has little effect on quality. In a study of the effects of freezing on tenderness, flavor, and juiciness (Arrington and Palmer, 1969), the frozen meat was found to be slightly less tender when baked or boiled and less juicy when baked. There was no significant difference in flavor, although the frozen meat appeared to have slightly less flavor than fresh meat. The overall effects of freezing were not considered objectionable.

BIOLOGICAL MATERIAL FOR RESEARCH

Certain organs and tissues not remaining with the carcass at slaughter are useful as biological material in research: blood, eyes, brains, reproductive organs, and others may be processed and marketed for this purpose. The organs are carefully removed and usually frozen or processed according to required specifications. Procedures are quite technical and processing this material is usually not feasible in small slaughter plants. Utilization of these by-products, however, represents an efficient use of material that may otherwise be wasted or sold for less profit. Large slaughtering plants such as those which may be operated by a cooperative should investigate the opportunity for processing and marketing these items.

SLAUGHTERHOUSE WASTE

The profitable marketing of animals should involve the use of all marketable by-products. Heads, viscera, and feet from rabbit slaughter are normally discarded, especially by the small processing units. However, these materials have value as food for zoo animals, in the processing of pet food, or as fertilizer. The disposition of the wastes for these purposes is limited to that from larger plants where the volume of material justifies the necessary equipment or the delivery to a processing plant. In view of the desirability of marketing all by-products, the need to conserve all sources of food and feed, and the proper disposal of waste to avoid pollution, the processing of slaughterhouse waste should be considered.

RABBIT SKINS AND PELTS

Rabbit skins and pelts have been used for many years as fur, in the manufacture of felt, and for a variety of miscellaneous toys and other items. With the development of many synthetic fibers and imitation furs, the demand for pelts by furriers has decreased. Today there are few markets for furs in the United States. Whether or not the pelts from meat slaughtering should be saved and prepared for marketing will depend upon the market demand and value, the type and number of rabbits being slaughtered, and the time and facilities available for preparing the skins. It is unlikely that the small producer slaughtering his own animals will find it economically worthwhile to process the skins.

Rabbit skins and pelts vary widely in quality and value. The different types of fur characteristics have been indicated in the description of the different breeds. Skins from young of any breed are normally of poorer quality and of less value than those from adult animals. Those with dense fur, which is not easily removed from the skin, are most desirable.

Preparation of skins or pelts for market begins with the removal at slaughter. Care should be exercised to avoid cuts or tears, and body fat should not remain with the skin. As the pelts are removed, they are turned inside out, and, while still warm and moist, they are placed on wire stretchers or shapers with the front leg casings on one side. Shapers may be made from number 9 gauge galvanized wire (Fig. 10.5). The shapers should extend or expand the pelts to their full length, but should not stretch them out of shape. The rear legs of the skins should be fastened to the ends of the wire shapers with a clothespin or some other fastener. Pelts should then be hung in a well-ventilated drying area, but not in direct sunlight. After the skins are dry the wire shaper is removed. Salt or other chemicals should not be used on skins, but as they are being packed for storage or shipment, some naphthelene (moth crystals) or paradichlorobenzene may be added as an insect repellent.

Trade journals and magazines frequently carry advertisements

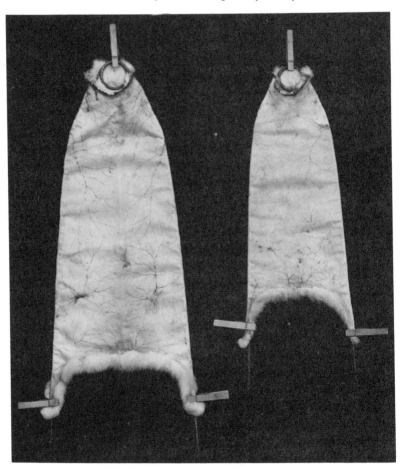

Fig. 10.5. Rabbit skins on shapers for drying. (Photo courtesy U.S. Department of Agriculture.)

regarding the purchase or sale of rabbit skins. These will usually specify the type of skin desired, and contact with the possible purchaser can provide additional information on methods for processing and shipping.

ANGORA WOOL

Angora rabbits formerly were raised primarily for their wool or fur which can be used to weave a valuable and prized fabric. Presently there is little if any commercial production, but some interest continues in the wool as a specialty item, and Angora rabbits are also raised for show or fancy. During the last world war, peak production of about 120,000 pounds of wool per year was reached. The average yield per rabbit per year is about 260 grams (9 ounces), but in Europe higher yields are reported from some strains.

The wool consists of long guard hairs and shorter, more dense undercoat fibers which are crimped. The hair may be clipped or sheared, or wool may be plucked when rabbits molt about three or four times a year, when hairs are 3–3 1/2 inches long. These methods are time consuming and result in high labor cost. A chemical method of "shearing" sheep is presently being studied and may have some promise for use with rabbits. The chemical is administered orally and causes an interruption of cell growth of the fibers near the skin so that the hair is easily broken at that point and the fleece can be pulled or rolled away. The chemical has not been approved and released for general use and apparently has not been used on rabbits.

RABBIT MANURE

Rabbit manure has value as a fertilizer, and it can be a valuable by-product of rabbit production. Depending upon the size of rabbitry and its methods of operation, it may be economically feasible to collect and dispose of the manure as fertilizer. It has no special chemical properties different from other animal manures, but it compares favorably with that of other animals.

Composition of rabbit manure and that from cattle and poultry is indicated in Table 10.3. The values for fertilizing constituents in the rabbit manure were determined on samples of mixed feces and urine from rabbits which were fed a commercial pelleted feed containing 15.5 per cent protein. The poultry and rabbit manures listed contained no bedding or litter, but that from cattle contained some bedding.

The fertilizing value of animal manures varies depending upon the species of animal, type of ration fed, amount of moisture present, amount of bedding or litter, and the method of handling

TABLE 10.3 COMPOSITION OF MANURE (%)[a]

	Organic Matter	Nitrogen	Phosphorus		Potassium	
			as P	as P_2O_5	as K	as K_2O
Rabbit	82.5	3.71	1.33	3.05	3.47	4.18
Cattle		2.90	0.72	1.65	2.14	2.58
Poultry		4.70	1.58	3.63	1.03	1.24

SOURCE: Values for cattle and poultry manure calculated from data by F. B. Morrison, 1957, *Feeds and Feeding*, Morrison Publishing Co.: Ithaca, N.Y.
a. Dry matter basis. Rabbit and poultry manure contained no bedding or litter. Cattle manure included bedding.

or storage. Manure may be used when fresh, but the nitrogen is fast acting and may "burn" the plants, although rabbit manure "burns" less than that from poultry. There is less nutrient loss, however, if it is applied to the soil when fresh. If allowed to decompose, some nitrogen will be lost, and if stored in the open exposed to rain, there will be additional losses from leaching. Composting the manure with materials such as grass cuttings, leaves, or other plant materials can prevent much of the nutrient loss. In some localities it may be more desirable to dry the manure and market it in small quantities.

If the collection and disposal of manure as fertilizer appears desirable, it is recommended that information regarding methods of handling, markets, and usage in a particular locality be sought from county or state extension personnel.

Some rabbit producers make a practice of raising earthworms in manure bins under rabbit cages. The worms aid in converting the manure to a desirable form for fertilizer, and some of the worms may be sold as fish bait. Flies do not reproduce in active worm beds and manure odor is reduced. The use of worm beds, however, requires moisture and this is undesirable in the rabbit house. It is recommended that manure be removed from the rabbit house to another area for the worm beds. Good sanitation practices require that manure be removed regularly.

REFERENCES

Arrington, L. R., and A. Z. Palmer. 1969. A comparison of the palatability of fresh and frozen rabbit carcasses. Fla. Agri. Expt. Sta. Mimeo Report AN 69–8.

Bingham, A. N. 1970. Commercial rabbit production. Ag. N. Ireland 45: 432–35.

Davis, J. W. C. 1968. Some aspects of large scale rabbit production. J. Inst. Anim. Tech. 19: 121–31.

DiLella, T., and L. Zicarelli. 1969. Meat production of New Zealand White rabbits. 2. Data on slaughter at various ages. (Text in Italian, English summary.) Atti. Soc. Ital. Sci. Vet. 23: 548–52.

Ferrera, B., T. DiLella, and L. Zicarelli. 1969. Meat production of New Zealand White rabbits. 1. Growth rate and food conversion index. (Text in Italian, English summary.) Atti. Soc. Ital. Sci. Vet. 23: 543–48.

Hardy, T. M. P., and E. H. Dolnick. 1948. Angora rabbit wool production. Circular 785. U.S. Department of Agriculture: Washington, D.C.

Haubold, W. 1974. Studies on carcass and meat quality of rabbit broilers of different breeds and crossbreeds. 1. Carcass quality of rabbit broilers. (Text in German, English summary.) Monatsh. Veterinarmed. 29: 343–51.

Kellogg, C. E., and G. S. Templeton. 1948. Effects of various factors on grades of New Zealand White rabbit skins. Circular 789. U.S. Department of Agriculture: Washington, D.C.

Lebas, F. 1969. Effect of starvation and transport on slaughter performance of rabbits aged 12 weeks. C. R. Acad. Agric. 55: 1007–10.

Parkin, R. J. 1972. Meat rabbit production. Agriculture (London) 79: 198–203.

Parkin, R. J., D. R. Jones, and E. Frost. 1973. Commercial rabbit production. Bull. Minist. Agric., Fish and Food (London) 50: 39pp.

Schlolaut, W. 1972. Aspects of fattening young rabbits. (Text in German.) Tierzuchter. 24: 287–89.

APPENDIX 1
OTHER SOURCES OF INFORMATION

Successful rabbit producers need information and help from a number of sources. Beginning producers need assistance in locating various supplies, breeding stock, markets, and processors. Established breeders want to be kept informed of new developments in the industry. The following agencies or organizations are recommended as sources of information, and producers are urged to make use of their assistance.

The United States Department of Agriculture publishes many types of printed matter related to rabbits and other animals. Lists of these bulletins and pamphlets and the publications themselves may be obtained from the Superintendent of Documents (U.S. Government Printing Office, Washington, D.C. 20402). County agricultural extension offices usually also have copies of these lists, which are periodically revised and up-dated.

Agricultural units of the land grant universities in each state may have available printed information and offer other services to the rabbit producer. Some of these universities conduct research with rabbits, and extension personnel may assist in procuring publications and in solving many problems. Contacts may be made through the county agricultural extension office. Short courses and workshops are often conducted at these universities.

Useful information regarding feeding and nutrition of rabbits is available from feed manufacturers and dealers, and they may assist with nutritional problems. Several of the larger feed manufacturers prepare and make available free bulletins concerned with rabbit raising.

State and local rabbit associations and clubs offer many opportunities for the exchange of helpful information. They promote rabbit shows and other activities on a local and statewide level. Information regarding supplies, breeding stock, and location of processors and markets can be obtained from these associations.

Several useful services are provided by the American Rabbit Breeders Association (present address: Office of the Secretary, 2401 E. Oakland Ave., Bloomington, Illinois 61701). It licenses official judges and registrars, maintains a registration system, and determines official breed standards. The association also publishes bulletins, a guidebook, and other materials related to rabbits. It cooperates with and assists state, county, and local associations and clubs, and sponsors an annual national show.

Journals, magazines, and periodicals on rabbits and other small animals publish much useful information. In addition, they carry classified and other advertisements which are useful in locating breeding stock, supplies, and possible markets for rabbits and their by-products.

References at the end of each chapter of this book should not be overlooked as sources of useful information. These are listed with respective chapters because they relate generally to material in that chapter. In some cases, however, the references, especially those at the end of the first chapter, are concerned with all phases of rabbit production.

APPENDIX 2
TABLES OF WEIGHTS AND MEASURES
AND TEMPERATURE CONVERSION

Weight
1 kilogram (kg)   2.205 pounds (avdp.)
                           35.275 ounces (avdp.)
1 gram (g)   1/1000 or .001 kilogram
                           .03527 ounces (avdp.)
1 milligram (mg)   1/1000 or .001 gram
1 pound (lb)   453.6 grams
                           .4536 kilograms
                           16 ounces
1 ounce (oz)   28.35 grams

Volume
1 liter (l)   .2642 gallons (U.S.)
                           1.057 quarts (U.S.)
                           2.113 pints (U.S.)
                           33.81 ounces, fluid (U.S.)
1 milliliter (ml)   1/1000 or .001 liter
                           .0338 ounces, fluid (U.S.)
                           14 drops
1 gallon (U.S.)   3.785 liters
1 quart (U.S.)   .946 liters
                           946 milliliters
1 pint (U.S.)   473 milliliters
                           16 ounces, fluid (U.S.)
1 ounce, fluid (U.S.) 29.57 milliliters
                           2 tablespoons (approx.)

1 tablespoon	3 teaspoons
	14 milliliters (approx.)
	1/2 ounce, fluid (U.S.)
1 teaspoon	4.7 milliliters
	60 drops (approx.)

Length
1 kilometer (km)	1000 meters
	.6214 miles
1 meter (m)	1.094 yards
	3.281 feet
	39.37 inches
1 centimeter (cm)	1/100 or .01 meters
	.394 inches
1 millimeter (mm)	1/1000 or .001 meters
	.0394 inches
1 mile	1.609 kilometers
1 yard	.914 meters
1 inch	2.54 centimeters

Temperature Conversion

Degrees Fahrenheit	Degrees Centigrade
110	43.3
100	37.8
90	32.2
80	26.7
70	21.1
60	15.5
50	10.0
40	4.4
32	0
30	−1.1
20	−6.6
10	−12.2
0	−17.8

Rabbit body
temperature: 101.5–104.1   38.6–40.1

To convert degrees Fahrenheit to Centigrade, subtract 32 and multiply by 5/9.

To convert degrees Centrigrade to Fahrenheit, multiply by 9/5 and add 32.

APPENDIX 3
TANNING SKINS

Rabbit skins have many uses and the variety of uses may be expanded by tanning. The process converts the raw hide or skin into a form of leather and imparts different properties to the pelt. It preserves the skin, makes it more pliable, durable, and resistant to water, and may impart a different color, depending upon the process used. Skins from rabbits are not tanned commercially as are cattle hides, but they are tanned for home use and for handcraft work.

Formerly, tanning was accomplished primarily by treatment with tannins extracted from the bark of certain trees. These materials are still used, but other chemicals and synthetic tanning products have replaced many of the vegetable tannins. The natural tannins may impart a desirable color. A much longer time is required for tanning with vegetable products than with chemicals. In the process, the tannic acid or other chemicals used precipitate collagen in the hide and combine with the protein of the skin to form the product known as leather. In making leather from hides of cattle or other large animals, the hair is removed, but in tanning skins of small animals, the hair normally remains.

Many different processes and treatments may be used for tanning, and no one procedure can be considered best for all conditions. Quality of the finished product will depend upon several factors. The type and preparation of the raw skin, the process used, length of time, temperature of the solution in some treatments, and other factors can affect results. The beginner may need to experiment with several methods to find the most satisfactory procedure. With practice and experience, the quality of tanned hides can be improved.

219

The two procedures described here have been used successfully for home tanning of rabbit skins. Chemicals required should be obtained from a chemical supplier, a local pharmacy, or possibly from a specialty shop supplying handcraft items.

PREPARATION OF SKINS

Regardless of the method to be used for tanning, proper preparation of the skin is an important step. Basically this involves softening, removal of the adhering fat and flesh, and removal of oil in the skin. The skin should be opened with a midline cut along the ventral or belly side so that it may be stretched on a flat surface. Adhering flesh and fat should be scraped away with a blunt knife or similar object. All oil should be removed for proper tanning, so working the skin in gasoline or other fat solvent is desirable to remove the last traces of fat. At slaughter, the skins are normally inverted (skin out) and placed on a shaper for drying. The dry skin should be softened by soaking in several changes of water for about 1–3 hours. Time required for softening will vary; soaking should not be longer than necessary since excessive soaking will tend to loosen the hair. Addition of borax or bicarbonate of soda (about 1 ounce per gallon) will aid softening, and a little soap or detergent will aid in removal of the fat.

SALT-ALUM TANNING

The solution for this process is prepared as follows:

A. Dissolve 1 pound (454 grams) of ammonium aluminum sulfate or potassium aluminum sulfate (alum) in 1 gallon (3.8 liters) of water.
B. Dissolve 4 ounces (115 grams) of sodium carbonate and 8 ounces (230 grams) of sodium chloride (salt) in 1/2 gallon (2 liters) of water.
C. Slowly add the soda-salt solution to the alum solution with vigorous stirring.

D. Mix flour with the combined solutions to make a thin paste, first mixing the flour with a little water to aid in preventing lumps.

The skin, prepared as previously described, should be stretched and tacked to a flat surface. Coat the skin with a layer of the paste about 1/8 inch thick and cover lightly with paper or cloth. Allow this to stand for about 24 hours, remove the paste, and apply a second coating. A third treatment may be required for thick skins. The last coating should remain for 3–4 days. Remove the paste and wash skin in a solution of borax or soda (1 ounce per gallon of water). Squeeze out (do not wring) excess solution; rinse in plain water and squeeze out excess. Stretch, and when nearly dry, work the skin by rubbing and pulling over the edge of a table, as in polishing shoes with a cloth, in order to soften the skin. If the skin is rough, it may be sanded with a coarse sandpaper block. A thin coating of neat's-foot oil, glycerin, or other leather conditioner may be applied.

This process is considered slightly better than the salt-acid method, but the finished product is usually harder and more working may be required to make it pliable. It may be necessary to soak the skin again, dry partially, and repeat the rubbing in order to make it pliable. Tanning may also be accomplished by soaking the skin for 2–4 days in the solution before addition of the flour. This amount of solution should be adequate for 3 or 4 rabbit skins.

SALT-ACID TANNING

The solution for this method is prepared as follows:

A. Dissolve 1 pound (454 grams) of sodium chloride (salt) in 1 gallon (3.8 liters) of water.

B. *Carefully* add 1/2 ounce (about 15 ml) of concentrated sulfuric acid to the salt solution. (Caution: sulfuric acid is very corrosive and must be handled with care. Avoid contact with skin or clothing. Store acid and the finished solution in glass or earthen containers—never metal.) When adding acid to the salt solution, pour in slowly with constant stirring. If the acid or mixture contacts the skin, rinse immediately with a solution of bicarbonate of soda.

C. Addition of the acid generates heat; the solution is ready for use when it has cooled.

Skins to be treated by this method should be prepared in the manner previously described. Place the skin in the salt-acid solution so that it is fully covered and allow it to remain for 1–3 days with periodic stirring. Remove, rinse in plain water then in a solution of borax or soda (1 ounce per gallon of water), followed by another water rinse. Squeeze out excess water, stretch, allow to partially dry, then treat the skin as described in the salt-alum method.

OTHER TANNING METHODS

Skins may be tanned with vegetable tannins, certain chromium salts, and other synthetic tanning materials. The procedure using vegetable tannin normally requires a long period for satisfactory results. Tanning with chromium salts (chrome tan) is a method widely used in the commercial manufacture of leather.

Materials for tanning may be obtained from certain biological supply companies or handcraft shops. Procedures for tanning using different chemicals will vary and instructions should accompany the materials marketed for tanning.

INDEX*

*Page references in italics indicate tables, figures, or other illustrations.

223